PHOTO QUEST

DISCOVERING YOUR
PHOTOGRAPHIC & ARTISTIC VOICE

Photography Books and Illustrated Online Classes by Rick Sammon

Recent Photography Books

Creative Visualization for Photographers
Evolution of an Image
Exploring Photographic Exposure
The Route 66 Photo Road Trip with Susan Sammon
The Oregon Coast Photo Road Trip with Susan Sammon

Illustrated KelbyOne Online Classes

Uncovering the Magic of the Rainforest: Costa Rica
Uncovering the Magic of Utah's National and State Parks
Uncovering the Magic of Yellowstone and Grand Tetons
Improving Your Creative Vision by Getting It Right in Camera
The 20 Time-Proven Rules of Composition
Rick's Top Tips for Taking Incredible Travel Photos
Breathtaking Bird Photography
Composition: The Strongest Way of Seeing
How to Stay Motivated in Photography
Transform Your Home into a Professional Photo Studio – Part I
Transform Your Home into a Professional Photo Studio – Part II
Capturing the Wild: Safari Photography

Words-Only Photography Book

Photo Therapy Motivation and Wisdom – Discovering the Power of Pictures

PHOTO QUEST

DISCOVERING YOUR
PHOTOGRAPHIC & ARTISTIC VOICE

RICK SAMMON
AND THE ALL-STAR PHOTO MENTORS

Cover design by Ivica Jandrijevic
Interior layout and design by www.writingnights.org
Book preparation by Chad Robertson
Edited by Cindy Snyder, Bob Sammon and Susan Sammon

ISBN: 979-8-6433-2415-7
Library of Congress:
LIBRARY OF CONGRESS CATALOGING-IN-PUBLICATION DATA:
NAMES: Sammon, Rick, author
TITLE: Photo Quest – Discovering Your Photographic & Artistic Voice
DESCRIPTION: Independently Published, 2020
IDENTIFIERS: ISBN 9798643324157 (Perfect bound) |
SUBJECTS: | Non-Fiction | Photography | Philosophy |
Motivation | Inspiration | Travel Photography
CLASSIFICATION: Pending
LC record pending

Printed in the United States of America.
Printed on acid-free paper.

24 23 22 21 20 19 18 17 8 7 6 5 4 3 2 1

This book is dedicated to you, the reader, because you have made the commitment, which will not be easy at times, to search for your artistic voice—no matter what your creative field or fields.

With practice, perseverance and most importantly passion I am sure you will find your artistic and creative voice.

I'm rooting for you.

An artist cannot fail; it is a success to be one.
— CHARLES COOLEY

Live to express, not to impress.
— UNKNOWN

The job of the artist is always to deepen the mystery.
— FRANCIS BACON

CONTENTS

FOREWORD
BY RICHARD BERNABE

My friend Rick Sammon is somewhat of a modern-day Renaissance man. He has a multitude of passions and interests and he can do so many things. What's infuriating to those of us who know him is just how well he does all of them! That includes, of course, the art and craft of photography, of which he is one of the all-time greats.

Rick often says he doesn't specialize in any particular photography genre and if you take a quick glance at his portfolio of wide-ranging places and subjects, it's easy to believe. He's well known for saying he's a photographer who specializes in not specializing. He's not a landscape photographer, nor a wildlife photographer. He's not a portrait, travel, music, nor bird photographer—not exclusively anyway. He's all those things and a lot more, including a mean guitar shredder and all-around super-nice guy.

As I said, he's a true Renaissance man.

I've never actually had a conversation with Rick about this particular subject, but if we did I'm sure he would say it's his desire to capture anything that inspires him or sparks a personal passion that's the driving force for his urge to create. We are all creators. As photographers, we look to the places and things we are passionate about for inspiration in creating images, just as the ancient Greeks consulted the muses to inspire art, song, poetry, and myth.

On the following pages of this book, you're going to read about the quest for your photographic and artistic voice and I believe that quest begins with deeply knowing yourself, your passions, desires, interests, and areas of intense curiosity. And while Rick's are obviously varied and diverse, mine are narrower in scope and almost exclusively include wild, exotic places and the people or creatures that inhabit them. But that's just me.

You might have different interests and life experiences that will help shape your own individual artistic voice. I simply don't waste time and creative energy attempting to photographically express subjects about which I am ambivalent. I've never photographed a wedding, for example. I never have and never will.

Katie Willard Virant, in a June 2018 *Psychology Today* article, "Art as Self-Care," explains: "When we're creating art, we are making decisions about what we like. What colors appeal to us? Which shapes are we drawn to? What textures do we enjoy? You may think you don't have any opinions on these questions, but you do! To make art is to make choices; to make choices necessitates paying attention to our inner selves as we assess which elements do and do not please us."

Great photographers and artists always create for themselves, not for others. They don't make photos for the sake of peer admiration or to avoid possible embarrassment and criticism from both professional online trolls and well-meaning colleagues. When you get right down to it, they are selfish.

All accomplished creative photographers are exceedingly selfish and self-centered, at least when it comes to their work. They only capture and create images of places and things that are deeply meaningful to themselves, and they express what they love in a way that resonates internally as well. That's the only thing they care about and that they should care about during the moment of the capture.

This selfishness, in an ironic way, leads to pure artistic selflessness.

A meaningful photograph is a creative expression of self and there is no greater gift a photographer can give their audience than a glimpse of their true inner personal vision. This is *constructive selfishness* and can help develop and amplify your unique artistic and photographic voice.

Then there's the dark side of selfishness too, of course. The internet and social media have been critical outlets for helping me grow professionally over the past fifteen years, as I was able to connect with more people and share my work and travel experiences from around the world with a bigger audience. I'm not even sure Rick and I would have become friends without the aid of social media, so I am certainly grateful for that as well.

But the internet, and social media in particular, is filled with potential traps and pitfalls for the creative, aside from being a massive time-killer. Sharing your work on sites like Instagram or Facebook leads to a popularity contest mentality where getting attention and "likes" becomes more important than your own personal vision. Soon, the collective tastes of your followers begin to shape the creative decisions you make with your camera instead of relying on what's important and meaningful to you.

Create solely for yourself. Ignore the critics on social media and the number of "likes" your work receives there and in photography forums. Ignore the positive or negative attention that other photographers receive. Ignore any stylistic trends or "in" places that the Internet heroes and their followers are flocking to at the moment. Ignore what's generally accepted as "good" or "bad" photographs and consider what's good or bad based on your own judgment and intuition.

All too often, our desire is to receive admiration from other people. We want to be liked and have our work validated by others. That's just being human. But critical acclaim and popularity are like a sugar high. It might feel good momentarily and swell your ego, but it soon dissolves away as the chase for more "likes" and a longer applause erodes your true creative impulses and inner photographic voice. This craving for more attention and dependency on the judgment of others is *destructive selfishness* and should be avoided at all costs, lest we lose that voice altogether.

So look deep inside for that voice from within, not from others, and adhere to the great Delphic maxim, *Know thyself.* And don't ever feel guilty about being selfish, at least as it applies to your photography. Both of the above principles, in my opinion, are essential to beginning that blissful quest to finding your true photographic voice.

There's no one better to help guide you down this creative journey than the "Renaissance Man" himself, Rick Sammon. You're in good hands, friends.

Enjoy the ride.

Richard Bernabe
Richardbernabe.com

PREFACE
ABOUT THIS BOOK

"**S**low down."

That was the best advice I ever received from a golf instructor, and I've had several. Once I slowed down, my golf game greatly improved.

"Slow down" is also good advice when learning how to play an electric guitar solo, because when you slow down, you not only hear the notes but the space between the notes, which is equally important.

"Slow down," in fact, is also good advice for all creatives: photographers, painters, moviemakers, stained-glass artists and so on.

What does all this have to do with this, my 41st book? Well, rather than having you be distracted by my photographs, as well as by the photographs of my awesome contributors, I want you to slow down and read the text slowly, carefully, and most importantly, thoughtfully.

You see, this book is about thinking about *your* photography and your art, and the next steps in your quest to reach the next level of creative image making. Put another way, a tripod, filter, lens, speedlite or other photo accessories (or a set of paints and paint brushes) can help you take better pictures (or make better paintings), but they may not make you a better photographer (or painter). There's a big difference, and that's where I hope you find this book comes in.

A photography or art book with no photographs or illustrations is not a new idea. In 1977 Susan Sontag wrote *On Photography*. A book without illustrations for artists is also not a new idea. In 1992 Julia Cameron published *The Artist's Way*. Both books are still bestsellers today (in 2020 as I write this).

On the pages of this book you will find some words of wisdom from me and from some of my photographer friends and mentors that will help you find your photographic and artistic voice. After all, we all need a voice if we want our photographic and artistic message to be heard and recognized.

Speaking of my photographer/artist friends, I could not have done this book without them. So, although my name is on the cover, this book is a collaboration with friends who want you to be the best you can be, photographically, artistically, and personally. What's more, we believe in the power of photography and art, and in the impact it can have on you and on others.

This book is a follow-up, a sequel if you will, to my previous book, *Photo Therapy Motivation and Wisdom – Discovering the Power of Pictures*. That book has no photographs. And like the book you are holding, *Photo Therapy* was written to provide motivation and inspiration.

Other similarities in the books are missions (assignments), which you will find at the end of each chapter, and quotes that drive home important concepts and most importantly, ideas for growth.

Also, like *Photo Therapy*, you don't necessarily need to read this book in chapter order. Each chapter stands alone. One idea is to read a chapter, take a break from this book, digest the ideas, make some creative photographs, and then come back and read another chapter.

Here is something else about this book: I actually did not have it in mind when I wrote *Photo Therapy*. It kind of happened on its own. I started jotting down some thoughts, talked with friends, did some research, began typing, and here we are!

Getting back to seeing my photographs, I do have several examples of some of my artistic images, along with how the image began (in-camera capture) which I would like to share with you. You can find them at ricksammon.com in my gallery named, What's Possible?

In that gallery, you will also find some of my photographs that were inspired by Rembrandt, Renoir, and Vermeer, well-known artists that followed their heart in creating their art.

So my friend, slow down and enjoy the journey—your quest—to finding your photographic and artistic voice, and maybe even a new part of yourself.

Rick Sammon
Croton on Hudson, New York
May 2020

ACKNOWLEDGEMENTS

First, I'd like to re-thank the photo mentors that contributed to this book. I learned a lot from these passionate pros, and I could not have written this book without their help and friendship.

Susan Sammon helped with this book in many ways, as she has helped with all my books and just about everything in my life since we were married in 1975.

Another Sammon also helped me with this book. My brother Bob, an excellent singer/songwriter/performer by the way, read the text and made changes and suggestions that improved the work.

Cindy Snyder was the final editor of this book. Thank you so much Cindy for reading through these 53,000+ words!

Chad Robertson, head of writingnights.org, made this book a reality, as he did with my *Photo Therapy* book. Chad took my Word document, edited it, formatted it, and got it on Amazon in a flash. In the world of Amazon self-publishing, Chad is "the man."

INTRODUCTION

Consider this: Think like a painter.

Painting, perhaps the most popular visual form or art, is basically an additive process: the painter adds paint to a canvas. Photography is basically subtractive: the photographer, through careful composition and cropping (or cloning in the digital darkroom), subtracts unwanted or distracting elements from a scene to create a vision—or impression—of a scene.

Sure, painters subtract, and photographers add, but the additive/subtractive analysis is mostly accurate.

Here is something else about painters: they think selectively, selectively controlling the brightness, shadows and highlights, contrast, color, sharpness, and so on, in a painting—every inch of the painting. Most painters would not consider a global adjustment (changing the entire image).

Painters also envision the end result, often starting with a medium (oils, pastels, etc.) that will convey their creative vision. They use what is commonly called, and what Ansel Adams called, "creative visualization."

Dorothea Lange shares another idea: "The camera is an instrument that teaches people how to see without a camera."

When photographers think like painters, photographing and processing images like an artist, images can look more creative and artistic. Here, too, creative visualization is the key.

Yes, we want to get the best in-camera image, but with Photoshop, Lightroom, and other imaging programs and plug-ins, we have the added benefit of being able to control every pixel in every inch within a file, and to add a painterly look to a digital file to create a work of art.

As photographers, painters, and illustrators, our ability to capture and shape light is one of the elements that makes or breaks an image. There are many master photographers, for example, from whom to learn lessons about light. More lessons can be learned about light by heading to a museum and studying master painters, sketchers, and sculptors.

For instance, Renaissance portrait painters, such as Leonardo da Vinci, shaped realistic anatomy using highlights and shadows to emphasize angles and fullness.

Speaking of highlights and shadows and Leonardo, my friend John Sinsheimer shared the following with me just a few days before I completed this book: To quote from Walter Isaacson's biography of Leonard da Vinci: "The first intention of the painter," Leonardo later wrote, "is to make a flat surface display a body as if modeled and separated from this plane, and he who surpasses others in this skill deserves most praise. This accomplishment, with which the science of painting is crowned, arises from light and shade, or may we say chiaroscuro."

Isaacson goes on to say: "Chiaroscuro, from the Italian for light/dark, is the use of contrasts of light and shadow as a modeling technique for achieving the illusion of plasticity and three-dimensional volume in a two-dimensional drawing or painting."

As you noted in your books: Light Illuminates and Shadows Define. Leonardo da Vinci would agree with you Rick!

Leonardo also used a technique called "sfumato" (a smoke-like effect) to add softness to his paintings, many of which have soft-edged subjects, as opposed to subjects having hard edges. Look at the lips and eyes of the Mona Lisa, for example. There are no hard edges. What's more, you will find soft/gradual transitions between the colors.

As an aside: When you are sharpening a photograph and trying to get the sharpest possible image, keep the sfumato technique (which you can somewhat simulate using the Gaussian Blur filter in Photoshop) in mind.

East Asian ink wash art used varying ink densities to provide shadows, capturing the spirit of the subject instead of a realistic reproduction. Impressionists, such as Monet, worked very quickly, emphasizing lighting patterns through the movement, tone, and shape of brushstrokes. Even the modern-day graffiti art of Banksy and the chalk art of Eduardo Rolero rely on key lighting edge placement to make 2D art-pop to perception-fooling 3D.

By examining the highlights and shadows in every art piece, it's possible to imagine the light source (the sun, a lamp, a reflection) and discern the proximity, strength, or additional sources.

By observing these details, you can better understand how each artist perceived light and its relationship to the subject, and light is the main element in every photograph you have ever taken or will take.

When it comes to seeing the effects of light on a subject, which will transfer to your photograph, there are six main things to see:

1. The **contrast range** in the scene, so you can determine if you need high dynamic range (HDR) photography, a flash, a reflector, or a diffuser (all of which compress the contrast range of a scene);

2. The **direction of light,** so you can see where shadows fall and where the light is reflected (remember that light illuminates and shadows define);
3. The **quality of light,** for a hard or soft photograph;
4. The **color of light,** for a warm or cool photograph;
5. The **Movement** of the light (as in moving water or the streaking taillight of a moving car), so you can choose a shutter speed to stop or blur movement/action; and
6. The technical and emotional **effects of shadows** in a scene, which can add to the separation of the elements in the scene to create a sense of separation of 3D elements in a 2D photograph, as well as create a dramatic or mysterious mood.

While you may find one artist whose style best matches your own aesthetic, you may also discover a variety of looks to experiment with when you are in different situations.

Spend some time looking at an artist's work and try to create a similar work of art. I tried to do that with my *Girl with a Pearl Earring* photograph that was based on Vermeer's painting, *Girl with a Pearl Earring*. If you want to see a comparison, do a Google search: Girl with a Pearl Earring Rick Sammon.

When you are thinking and working on an image, keep in mind that every artistic creation—in photography, music, painting, writing, and so on—starts with an idea. Often, an idea goes through several incarnations before it becomes a reality. The idea goes through an evolution, of sorts.

Let's take a look at Webster's definition of the word *evolution*: "The gradual development of something, especially from a simple to a more complex form…the process of gradual, peaceful and progressive change and development."

Now let's take a look at the keywords in that description, and how they apply to your photography and art.

Gradual—If you are new to digital photography or any art form, don't expect overnight results. Learning takes time; it's a gradual process. Try not to get frustrated when things don't turn out as planned and envisioned. Easy to say, I know, having been there and done that.

Peaceful—Oftentimes, we put ourselves under stress, especially when we are photographing, because we have to get the shot and will do almost anything to achieve our goal. Again, "been there, done that." I do find, however, that the more peaceful I feel when I am working on my images, the better the results. Listening to peaceful music, mostly the Tommy Emmanuel station on Spotify helps keep me mellow.

Progressive change and development—This is the cool part of the evolution of a photograph or work of art. You see your changes and development as a photographer. The more you learn, the more creative you become, and the better you get at photographing and processing.

Of course, sometimes and at some point in the stages of our evolution, we realize that our original idea was not that great to begin with, so we ditch it, or maybe our original idea takes on an unexpected, and even better reality.

The message here is to keep those ideas coming and try to be realistic about them.

YOUR MISSION
Think like a painter.

MEET YOUR ALL-STAR PHOTO MENTORS

I'd like to take a moment to introduce you to your **All-Star Photo Mentors** for this book. On the following pages these talented pros and I will try to help you find your photographic and artistic voice, as well as help you become a better photographer and artist.

I could not have produced this book without the help and support—and friendship and love—of these awesome photographers and photo mentors, each of whom has helped me in my personal quest to become a better photographer and creative.

Read their words of wisdom carefully, and please check out their websites. Follow them on social media and become their friends.

By the way, I came up with the idea of adding my talented friends' words of wisdom to this book after seeing Ringo Starr & His All Starr Band, and after hearing him sing "With a Little Help From My Friends" in Bethel, New York, in 2019.

Ringo was awesome, but his friends truly enhanced the experience, as I trust you will find my friends do in this book.

ALEC ARONS
Seeing and sharing through the lens of mindfulness.
photosbyagarons.com

ERIN BABNIK
Creative Coach
erinbabnik.com

SEAN BAGSHAW
A good person, husband, and father while
hopefully helping more than harming.
outdoorExposurephoto.com

RICHARD BERNABE
I create art for myself.
richardbernabe.com

MARTIN BAILEY
It's all about the journey!
martinbaileyphotography.com

ANNE BELMONT
Finding your inner heart through nature.
annebelmontphotography.com

SCOTT BOURNE
Light and shadows warrior.
picturemethods.com

STEVE BRAZILL
Music, Imagery & More
stevebrazill.com

JEFF CABLE
Sharing the passion of photography.
jeffcable.com

RON CLIFFORD
Inspirologist—helping photographers reach for their potential.
ronclifford.com

EDWARD COOLEY
Serial Entrepreneur, Scenic Photographer, Fine Art Print Maker.
edcooleyfineart.com

TONY L. CORBELL
Guided by Light and Shadow.
tonycorbell.com

PATRICIA DAVIDSON
Capturing the vibrant colors of the West.
patriciadavidsonphotography.com

SUSAN DIMOCK
*Psychotherapist/social worker turned photographer who enjoys the challenge
of creating meaningful and purposeful stories.*
susandimockphotography.com

DAVE DEBAEREMAEKER
Exploring the worlds at the edges of my imagination.
studiodave.ca

UNMESH DINDA
A teacher at heart.
youtube.com/piximperfect

FRANK DOORHOF
Why fake it when you can create it?
frankdoorhof.com

DARRELL GULIN
Teaching teaches the teacher.
gulinphoto.com

RANDY HANNA
Adventure crazed photographer, and self-effacing humorist.
randyhannaphotography.com

KAREN HUTTON
Purveyor of Awesomeness.
karenhutton.com

STEVEN INGLIMA
Dedicated to the craft of creation, in all of its forms.
smiphotos.com

LOU JONES
Photography has designed my life.
panAFRICAproject.org

KEN KAMINESKY
Awesome life experience facilitator.
discoveryPhotoTours.com

SCOTT KELBY
*Bestselling photography book author, Photoshop and Lightroom Guy,
co-host of "The Grid," and struggling guitar player.*
kelbyone.com

DON KOMARECHKA
Mad Scientist.
donkom.ca

JULIE LEE
Photographer and educator, celebrating nature with a camera.
julieleephoto.com

LINDA D. MARSHALL
Each of us has a special gift.
lindamarshall.org

ALEX MORLEY
Striving for perfection.
alexmorleyphoto.com

MICHAEL PACHIS
*I aspire to make photographs that look into an animal's eyes
and reflect the mind looking into the lens.*
mpachis.com

JUAN PONS
I see through the eyes of my wild subjects.
juanpons.org

IAN PLANT
Dedicated to educating and inspiring others about the art of photography.
ianplant.com

PIPER MACKAY
Africa is the oxygen for my soul.
pipermackayphotography.com

SERGE RAMELLI
Bonjour mesdames et messieurs!
photoserge.com

TREY RATCLIFF
Eater of photography and taker of bacon.
stuckincustoms.com

GREG VAUGHN
I wander, searching for the wonders.
gregvaughn.com

ART WOLFE
Explore. Create. Inspire.
artwolfe.com

1.

WHAT MAKES SOMEONE AN ARTIST?

*"Every child is an artist. The problem is how
to remain an artist once he grows up."*
— PABLO PICASSO

I f you are a photographer, the first step on this creative journey of
yours is to ask yourself: "Am I an artist or a photographer?" If you
are a painter, you can ask yourself: "Do I just copy a painting or
idea, or do I create something unique?" If you are a musician, you can
ask yourself: "Am I creating original music or am I just plying 'covers'
(renditions of popular songs)? To answer that question, you first need
to ask: "What's the difference?"

We can begin to find the answer by looking at the difference between
art (which is subjective) and science (which is objective).

Art: An artistic photograph often has a sense of mystery, as discussed
in **Chapter 11: Creating a Sense of Mystery**. We can, of course, add,
"creating a sense of fantasy" when it comes to an artist's image.

Science: A straight, or "scientific." photograph if you will, simply
shows what we see without any digital enhancements—none whatsoever.

Therefore, as educator Karen P. L. Hardison (who writes for

enotes.com) states, "Art and science are therefore in fundamental character very dissimilar."

So, if we translate that to photography, there is a fundamental difference between being an artist and a photographer.

That being said, I have seen straight-out-of-the camera artistic images that have captivated me, as does art, simply because the photographer composed and exposed the photograph perfectly, but more importantly because of the subject—we should never underestimate the importance of a good subject. Think of the most beautiful sunset or sunrise photograph you have taken or have seen. Thanks to Mother Nature "painting" the scene with dramatic light and shadows, adding "brush strokes" of colorful light, and creating breathtaking clouds, we have, indeed, a work of art in a straight shot.

I can't stress enough the importance of a good subject. My friend/artist/photographer Art Wolfe agrees and has dozens of examples in his book, *Human Canvas*. In this coffee table book, Art uses his exceptional photography and his background in fine art painting to transform skin into an abstract landscape.

According to Art, "The project was inspired by the body-painting traditions of indigenous peoples that I have photographed worldwide, and particularly those in Ethiopia and Papua New Guinea. I set out to present my 'own take' on this art form and explore concepts of universal beauty.

Through the use of lines, patterns, textures, and unusual points of view, I tried to abstract the human form and create a unique and captivating look of the human body as art. The result, I feel, is an energized expression of both artistic mastery and cultural impact."

I like Art's idea and the way he explains it. An important point he mentions is that it's his "own take." I think if we experiment with a concept and try our "own take," we just may come up with an original—and artistic—idea.

When asking ourselves if we are an artist or a photographer, for example, there is another answer: you can be both.

I asked this question on Facebook and received dozens of comments. I used them here with the understanding of these Facebook friends that their comments would be used in a book.

Take a look, and see if you see yourself in these words, especially in the last two comments.

ERIN BABNIK

You could ask the same question of someone whose medium is paint: are they a painter or an artist? A professional house painter or sign painter might not self-identify as an artist, even if they take pride in having achieved a high level of craftsmanship. In my view, an artist is simply someone who uses their medium as an outlet for personal expression, intending to put something of them into each creation, no matter what medium they are using. A photographer has many options for expressing a personal way of 'seeing' that is infused with personal ideas about what is in front of the camera—from framing to timing to lighting to post-processing, the options are nearly limitless. Because I use cameras to suggest my ideas about the world, I consider myself an artist, but I am also a photographer.

RON CLIFFORD

My camera is the instrument of connection. Photoshop and Lightroom my studio. I am an artist. My medium is light.

BUDDY WEISS

The answer is "yes." I'm a photographer because I take photographs. I'm an artist because I select the subject, the camera position, the framing, the timing, the aperture and shutter speed, and because I make my desired adjustments in post-processing to convey a look and feel that is mine and mine alone. There you have it.

ALEC ARONS

To me it is about creating images with mood and feeling that I care about intending to express myself to others visually. So yes, I am an evolving artist that has selected photography as his method of expression.

BONNIE GRESHAM DAVIDSON

Sometimes I'm a photographer taking pictures as we travel. Sometimes I'm an artist creating images. These might be considered artistic by some and not by others. But the freedom of being an artist far outweighs what others think. We don't all have the same taste.

SHELLY ST. JEAN

My art starts in my mind, as a vision, I imagine it and then I work it into a real-life setup I use the beauty around me and maybe add more. My canvas is my camera where I paint with light to create. Therefore, I am not only a photographer, I am also an artist!

KEVIN SCOTT

I am both, depending on the situation. Sunrise/sunsets, I'm an artist. Sports, I'm a photographer. Weddings, I'm mostly a photographer. But to be honest, even wedding photos can delve into artistry, depending on what I may do in post. I hope this helps.

ERIC FRIEDMANN

I'm a photographer who occasionally makes art.

RICK BERK

I'm a photographic artist. Because I create with the camera a look that I want to convey to my viewer through the creative use of shutter speed and aperture.

GLENN TAYLOR

I'm not sure anymore. I just keep moving forward and trying to improve.

KAREN HOFFMAN

I am still learning and haven't reached that personal verdict yet.

I think the message here is that it's okay to be both a photographer and artist, or both a musician who plays original music or cover songs to, as my mother told me when I a kid, "Always follow your heart."

Hey, I know that is not always an easy choice, due to the ups and downs of growing as a photographer, artist, and person. I'll talk more about that in **Chapter 5: The Rollercoaster Ride of Creatives**.

The key is to never give up.

Ask yourself: "Am I an artist or a photographer (or both), or a creative or someone who just copies?" That question begs another question: "What is art?"

Seeking the answer will help us find our photographic and artistic voices.

Of course, art is subjective, but I think deep down inside we can tell the difference between a work of art and the "same old, same old." For example, I think Orson Welles' *Citizen Kane*, with its very dramatic lighting (accentuated by using black-and-white film) and unique camera angles, is a work of art. I think many film lovers would agree. At the opposite end of the creative spectrum are daytime soap operas on broadcast television channels. The lighting is relatively boring, among other factors. That being said, daytime soap operas are not intended to be works of art.

When it comes to music (one of my passions), the same idea holds: "bubble gum" pop songs like "Yummy Yummy Yummy" (the 1968 hit by the Ohio Express) are not works of art. Adagio for Strings by Samuel Barber is art. It was played at JFK's funeral, and some say it is the saddest classical piece ever written.

The following are a few of my favorite explanations of art by well-known artists.

> *Ideas alone can be works of art...All ideas need not be made physical...A work of art may be understood as a conductor from the artist's mind to the viewer's. But it may never reach the viewer, or it may never leave the artist's mind.*
> — SOL LEWITT

> *We all know that art is not truth. Art is a lie that makes us*

realize the truth.
— PABLO PICASSO

Art is filling a space in a beautiful way.
That's what art means to me.
— GEORGIA O'KEEFFE

Art is a habit-forming drug.
— MARCEL DUCHAMP

Art is a revolt, a protest against extinction.
— ANDRÉ MALRAUX

Expanding on André Malraux's quote about extinction, I think consciously or subconsciously, we would all like to leave something behind when we leave this world. That is why I can relate to the quote. Another way to convey that sentiment: an artist lives forever. Long live the artists!

On a side note, a writer also lives forever, which is kind of cool, because you can talk to people even after you are dead.

YOUR MISSION

Take a straight photograph of an everyday object, perhaps a piece or a bowl of fruit. In the digital darkroom, try adding some enhancements. Even a blurry vignette, which appears to change the depth of field, can make an image look more artistic. If you are a painter, try similar techniques.

2.

WHAT'S NEEDED ON THE PHOTO ARTIST'S PALETTE?

Creativity is allowing yourself to make mistakes.
Art is knowing which ones to keep.
— SCOTT ADAMS

What does it take to be a photo artist, or any type of artist for that matter? What's needed on the artist's palette? That's a challenging question to answer because there are many different types of art, and of course, art is subjective. But let's give it a whirl.

To begin, an artist needs to stand out from the crowd and do something different, something unique, and something compelling.

For example, several painters tried their brush at the Last Supper, but none are as notable as Leonardo da Vinci's masterpiece. There is, however, an exception. In *The Sacrament of the Last Supper*, Salvador Dalí, who was going through what he called his "Nuclear Mysticism" phase, created a unique and memorable painting of the historic event. These two paintings, as well as creative phases, are discussed in detail later on in this book.

Salvador Dalí thought "outside the box." He thought differently. This thought process set him apart from the crowd. He had the confidence to turn that thought process into a reality.

It's easy to give the advice: "Think outside the box." It's harder to develop totally new ideas, but it's not impossible. A starting point is to ask ourselves: "How can we add our unique touch to a subject that has been photographed or illustrated a million times, such as Mesa Arch in Utah?" Another question is: "What can I photograph or make a painting of that has not been photographed a million times, such as a remote area in Goblin Valley State Park, which is about two hours from Mesa Arch?"

Another way to look at thinking outside the box is to think about disrupting your traditional way of thinking. This concept is discussed in the best-selling book by Luke Williams, *Disrupt: Think the Unthinkable to Spark Transformation in Your Business.*

Yes, it is a business book, but I think the concept of thinking differently will also help you with your photography and photo quest. Or as Seth Godin, author of *Linchpin* says: "Don't let the title fool you. This book is stuffed with practical, useful ideas that will change the way you create and sell practical, useful ideas." What I like most about this quote is the phrase "the way you create."

Here's one example from the book that drives home the point of disruptive thinking: The author talks about a meeting of executives at a sock company. The executives want to do something different in the age-old sock business. One executive comes up with the idea of mismatched socks. The other executives think the idea is silly. The guy with the idea leaves the company and starts a mismatched sock company. All you need to do is a Google or Amazon search on mismatched socks to see the effect, and success, of thinking differently.

We'll talk more about the business side of photography and art in **Chapter 18: The Business of Being Creative.**

Here's an example of *not* thinking outside the box. Susan and I were running a photo workshop in Yosemite, known for its iconic locations and photographs of those locations, including Half Dome, made famous by Ansel Adams.

During the workshop, we received a cell phone call from one of the workshop participants. "I'm not getting the iconic shots," she said. I said, "Great! Now you can use your vision to create pictures you can call your own."

And speaking of pictures we can call our own, here's another workshop story. Susan and I had set up a workshop to photograph in the national parks in Utah: Bryce, Zion, and Arches. The day before the workshop, the United States government shut down all the national parks.

At first, the participants were unhappy. Susan and I made a plan to photograph in the lesser known parks and scenic areas, including Peek-A-Boo Slot Canyon and Goblin Valley State Park, as well as some areas around the national parks.

Guess what? The participants came away with unexpected pictures and had a wonderful time. The workshop exceeded their expectations. They were able to think outside the box, which was a challenging and rewarding experience.

Getting back to the question of what's needed on the artist's palette, I found some additional answers in an article by Christine Nishiyama on artplusmarketing.com about what she feels is necessary to be an artist (she is talking about drawing, although her philosophy applies to photography and other art forms, as well).

We'll first take a look at her advice on the "five core elements" needed to be an artist, and then see how it applies to photography, and whether the life (or even part-time life) of an artist is for you. Take it away Christine Nishiyama.

VISUAL LANGUAGE:	Being able to use lines, shapes, and colors to communicate.
PRODUCTIVITY + DISCIPLINE:	Being able to form and keep creative habits and produce a large amount of work.
CREATIVITY + IMAGINATION:	Being able to come up with original ideas.
SELF-AWARENESS AND EXPRESSION:	Being able to reflect on, learn about, and express ourselves.
COMMUNITY:	Being able to find and accept positivity, encouragement, and constructive feedback.

Now, let's take a look at how these points relate to photography and art.

VISUAL LANGUAGE—Through the use of creative composition, lighting, camera settings, lens selection, and of course, an interesting subject, we can tell a story without using words. Yes, a picture is worth many, many words. It's up to us to tell our own story and to convey our message.

Most often, photographs or painting of a subject in an environment tell more of a story than a tight shot. That is why I like to take environment travel portraits—pictures of subjects in their environment—rather than lots of headshots, which often don't offer a clue as to where the photograph was taken.

One example of going wide with photographic composition is *Tank Man*, which shows an unidentified rebel standing alone in front of four army tanks in Tiananmen Square during the protests in 1989.

That being said, an extreme close-up can also tell a story. One example is a photograph of the head of an insect poking its head out of the clutches of a Venus flytrap.

Before you take a picture or begin a painting, consider your storyline and what your picture will say to the viewer. Consider your voice.

PRODUCTIVITY + DISCIPLINE—Ernest Hemmingway summed up productivity in a few words: "Never confuse movement with action." Here's another way to convey that idea: Stop spinning your wheels.

As photographers and artists, we need to grow. We can't keep doing the "same old, same old." If we do, we grow stale or, when you get to my age (almost seventy as I write this book) you become a dinosaur. For me, that's probably one of the worst things I could hear, which is one reason I actively pursue new ideas and give myself challenges, such as writing a photography book with no photographs or only one photograph, and going to the ends of the earth (including Antarctica and the High Arctic) to make new pictures.

So how do we avoid becoming a dinosaur? The answer is that we must keep it fresh. When it comes to our photography and art, we need to experiment with new techniques.

Following are some ideas about how you can avoid mistaking motion for action when it comes to photography, but you can see how these concepts apply to other art forms, as well.

Give yourself an assignment, maybe one that lasts a week or a month. Challenge yourself to work more with shadows, or only take a 50mm lens when you go photographing.

In Photoshop or Lightroom, just for the fun of it, try a new processing technique, such as making the most dramatic black-and-white image you can, boosting the contrast to the point where your images "pops" off the screen, yet still retains details in the highlight and shadow areas.

Another photo idea is to join a photo workshop that takes you out of your comfort zone. If you like landscape photography, take a city/street photography workshop. My guess is that you will be able to apply many of the techniques you use in street photography to your landscape photography, including creative composition and looking for color and contrast in a scene. You will probably see other similarities; including that successful street photographers and landscape photographers need to have that all-important individual voice.

Katharine Hepburn summed up discipline so eloquently: "Without discipline, there's no life at all."

Discipline and productivity go hand in hand when it comes to the artist's life. Some people I know have built-in discipline, getting up around 6:00 a.m. each day because they feel they must produce, must create, must not become a dinosaur. They also must plan the day so there is exercise time and break time, because as the saying goes, "all work and no play make Jack a dull boy."

When it comes to photographic and artistic discipline, again, productivity is important. One idea is to discipline yourself to take a different type of picture of the same subject each day. You can start in the morning by photographing or painting a picture of your coffee or teacup. Try capturing the steam rising from the cup at different angles, photograph toward and away from the main light source in your kitchen. You may be surprised at how different the steam looks when photographed, painted, and seen at different angles.

If you'd like to be more disciplined, Entrepreneur.com offers (and expands on) these ten ideas:

1) Know your weaknesses. We all have weaknesses.
2) Remove temptations. Like the saying goes, "out of sight, out of mind."
3) Set clear goals and have an execution plan.
4) Build your self-discipline.
5) Create new habits by keeping it simple.
6) Eat often and healthy.
7) Change your perception of willpower.
8) Give yourself a backup plan.
9) Reward yourself.
10) Forgive yourself and move forward.

One simple way to be more disciplined is to make a checklist of things you'd like to do, and then make sure you check off those items each day.

If you need help making and sticking to a checklist, it's apps to the rescue. Many apps are available for your smartphone and computer that will help you plan your day, week, month, or year. You just need the discipline to check the app. ☺

CREATIVITY AND IMAGINATION—You may have heard the saying: "The creative adult is the child who survived." How true is that? As adults, we must use our imagination, as we did when we were kids, to express our ideas and ourselves.

Earlier in this chapter, I talked about doing the "same old, same old" thing. To break that habit, we must take risks; we must do something new and innovate, even if it's only new to us. That is how we grow as a photographer, artist, and person.

Taking risks invites getting criticism. We'll deal with that topic in **Chapter 8: Criticisms: The Good, The Bad, and the Ugly**. But for now, my best advice is to follow your heart, and not to take all negative comments about your photography and art to heart.

Albert Einstein said, "Imagination is more important than knowledge." Again, those words ring true. However, the more technical skill we have as photographers—knowing what our camera and image-processing software programs can and can't do—will help us photographically create the images we see in our mind's eye.

Knowing the rules of composition, when it comes to photography, painting, and music, is also important. Equally important is to know when to break the rules. As Edward Weston said, "To consult the rules of composition before making a picture is a little like consulting the law of gravitation before going for a walk."

A painter knows how colors interact and reflect light and draw attention to a subject in a scene. A painter also knows how to create a sense of scale and depth in a painting, and more.

As photographers and artists, we need to know about color, light, scale, depth, and more to create an image of which we can be proud—so proud that if we were a kid, we'd hang it on the refrigerator door.

There are many ways to learn about these all-important elements in photography and art: books, online classes, seminars, and websites. Research these topics. The more you put in, the more you will get out.

SELF-AWARENESS AND EXPRESSION—In my seminars and photo workshops, I talk about photo-emotional intelligence and situational awareness.

The idea of photo-emotional intelligence is to know our effect on other people. We must be aware—have self-awareness—of how our actions, expression, body language, tone of voice, and so on, affect those around us. This is especially important when taking pictures of people in distant lands, but it's also important when working with a model in the studio.

The idea of situational awareness is almost the opposite of photo-emotional intelligence: we have to be aware of everything that is going on around us. This is especially true when our attention is focused on the image in the viewfinder or on the back of a camera or smartphone. If we are aware of what might come into the frame, to ruin or make the picture even better, we can change our composition to tell a different story. If we have situational awareness, and if we know how to quickly change a camera setting, we can make instant decisions that may result in a better-than-planned shot.

At my events, I also talk about "gesture"—the gesture of the subject in a photograph. It's the gesture that adds to the "expression" of the photograph, and it is how you capture that expression that makes it your photograph.

When it comes to photographs and paintings of people, hand gestures are important, which is why dictators use strong hand gestures when they speak, and why religious leaders use soft and calming hand gestures when they give a sermon.

We also see gestures in clouds and waves, and it's those gestures that can be strong or calming. Here, too, how you capture those gestures (using short or long exposures, for example) helps you tell your story of the scene. It's how you express your vision.

COMMUNITY—What I am about to say will sound egotistical until I explain. Here goes: I have no competition. My explanation is summed up in this quote by Maryam Hasnaa: "Confidence isn't thinking you are better than everyone else, it's realizing that you have no reason to compare yourself to anyone else."

Picasso, Rembrandt, Vermeer, Renoir, and the other master painters had no competition, even though they might have thought they did at the time. Likewise, Ansel Adams, Dorothea Lange, Richard Avedon, Diane Arbus, and other master photographers had no competition, even though they might have thought they did at the time.

The idea here is that all the aforementioned artists had an individual style, an individual voice. They had loyal followers, some of whom followed other artists.

If today's photographers/artists feel as though they have competition, it may stifle their work because they may feel threatened, which is a negative feeling. That can harm the artist. One extreme example: Van Gogh cut off his ear lobe in a fit of mania after getting in a fight with fellow artist Paul Gauguin.

On the other hand, if photographers share what they know, especially on social media sites, they will not only grow as photographers (getting feedback), but they will also grow the number of their fans because they are so giving with their knowledge. My friend Scott Kelby, head of KelbyOne.com, is one such example of a giving person.

Sure, KelbyOne charges for online training, but the stuff they give away for free (including the weekly web TV show *The Grid*) is amazing.

By being social, by giving stuff away for free, photographers become part of a community, a worldwide community. That community, which includes online forums, can not only be a source of inspiration but a source of income, because you will be involved in a community of people who may want to take a workshop, attend a seminar, buy a book or video, or purchase an online class.

So, join the community and share and share alike. Don't be a hermit, keeping all your secrets to yourself.

As Maryam Hasnaa pointed out in a few paragraphs ago, having confidence is important. Here are just a few of my suggestions on how to build CONFIDENCE in your *everyday* life.

C—Coach Vince Lombardi said, "**Confidence** is contagious. So is the lack of confidence." Try to project confidence. This can be accomplished with body language and the tone of your voice.

O—Be **optimistic**. "Optimism is the faith that leads to achievement," Helen Keller said. "Nothing can be done without hope and confidence." Think about how fortunate you are. Look for the good in things and not the bad.

N—Wear something **new** and different, something that will draw attention to you and that will require you to respond to a comment. Don't be shy. At one Christmas party at our house, I wore my Yellow Submarine (from The Beatles movie of the same name) sneakers—and they were a hit.

F—**Find** a group to join and offer to share your expertise. Telling honest stories about you is a good way to feel better about yourself.

I—**Introduce** yourself to a stranger, even if it's the person at the post office or supermarket. You might be surprised at the smile you bring to a stranger's face.

D—Take the **Dale Carnegie** course on Effective Communications and Human Relations. As mentioned elsewhere in the book, taking the course was the best business decision I ever made.

E—**Explore** a new path. Go someplace that you have never gone before. Getting lost can be fun.

N—Avoid **negative** people. Think positive.

C—Be **calm**. Confidence and calmness go together. Try not to get upset at criticisms.

E—Do something **exciting**, challenging and rewarding, even if it's as simple as making a pie.

Okay, let's take a look at some suggestions for building CONFIDENCE in your photography and artistic life...and in your creative photo quest.

C—**Create** something *you* like, in-camera and with Photoshop or Lightroom or with plug-ins. The same goes for a painting. Let your imagination go wild.

O—Go **online** and see what famous photographers and artists are doing. Copy an idea and be proud that you were successful.

N—Take a **new** picture every day or make a new sketch every day. Photograph or sketch something that you never photographed or sketched before. Need some inspiration for a hand photograph or sketch? Do a Google image search for "Leonardo da Vinci's hands."

F—**Find** your passion. Ask yourself what pleases you the most photographically and artistically. Learn as much about that subject as possible and apply that knowledge to your photography. (Leonardo da Vinci dissected cadavers to learn about how muscles and bones affected the surface of the skin.)

I—Improve your knowledge of photographic and artistic techniques. Study light, composition, the exposure triangle, depth of field, color, and so on, and apply this knowledge to the image you see in your mind's eye.

D—Just do it. I know it's easier said than done but take a leap of faith and just do it. Imagine that you are standing at the edge of a high diving board. You look down. The longer you look and the longer you wait, the harder it will be to…just do it. FYI: The phrase "Just do it" belongs to Nike.

E—Know your **equipment**. Know your camera controls and know what your camera can and cannot do. Learn how to operate your camera in the dark, which will come in handy for pre-sunrise and low-light shots. Also learn about accessories, such as filters and speedlites, and explore how they can improve your photography. The same idea applies to painting when it comes to brushes, paints, canvasses, and so on.

N—Never stop learning. As the Buddhists say, learning is health. Keep on learning and stay healthy—mentally and physically. They are connected, as Dr. John E. Sarno points out in his wonderful book (which helped cure me of crippling back pain), *Healing Back Pain: The Mind-Body Connection*.

C—Ask for constructive **criticism**. Post a photo or a photo of a painting on social media and ask for constructive criticism. Or post two photos/paintings in one graphic and ask which one the viewer prefers. You'll start a dialog and will learn from the experience. I have found that when I post two images in one graphic and ask for feedback, many more people respond than when I just post a single photo.

E—Exhibit your work. My guess is that there is a coffee shop or library in your area that hosts photo and painting exhibits. Make a few prints and have an exhibit. Offer to give a talk on your photography and art. If you do this, use photographs of local scenes as opposed to faraway places like Antarctica or Mongolia. I think most photographers will tell you that local art sells more than photos of exotic locations.

Confidence is important, but so is COMMITMENT.

Take a look at these suggestions, and keep them in mind on your creative photo quest:

C—**Carve** out some time every day to learn something new. I am a firm believer that if you want to do something, you will find the time.

O—Keep this saying in mind: **Onward** and upward. My dad would end his emails with this well-known phrase. He kept encouraging me to be positive. Those daily words helped when I was feeling down.

M—Be **mindful** of your creative decisions. As Ernest Hemmingway once said, "Never confuse movement with action." Be mindful that you are making progress and not just spinning your wheels.

M—**Meditate.** Actual meditation is good, but you can mediate by mowing the lawn, playing a musical instrument, cooking, and so on, if you get in "the zone." Try to silence the noise in your brain.

I—Get **inspired**. Look at the work of other photographers and artists. Go to museums and art galleries. Join a photo workshop. Inspiration is everywhere…if you look for it. As the Good Book says, "Seek and ye shall find."

T—Think **tenacity**. Be firm/strong when it comes to believing in your ideas. Have courage. Believe in yourself.

M—Follow your **mission** statement. Write a mission statement that expresses your work and your philosophy. Take your time. Run your mission statement by some family members and friends and ask for their input. Viewers of your website will identify you with your mission statement.

E—**Evaluate** your work. Take a good, honest look at your work. You will find more on this topic in **Chapter 15: Analyze This**.

N—**Never** say "Never" and never procrastinate. I know it's easier said than done, but never give up. Keep in mind that rejections are part of the photographer's and the artist's life.

We all get down from time to time, even well-known artists. Here's one example: Impressionist painter Claude Monet struggled with depression later on in his life. He wrote: "Age and chagrin have worn me out. My life has been nothing but a failure, and all that's left for me to do is to destroy my paintings before I disappear."

Well, lucky for us, Monet never gave up and painted until the end of his life.

T—Keep up with **technology**. As much as some of us may resist it, we need to keep up with technology. Photoshop, Lightroom, and plug-ins can help us awaken the artist within. We may realize that a feature can help us, or we may discover a feature by accident.

What's more, new technology can make our old pictures look better, or as my friend Art Wolfe said about the slides he shot in the 1980s compared to his digital files of the 2000s: "I can't believe how soft my slides are compared to my digital files."

There are at least two more things (at least) on the list of what it takes to be an artist—and to find your photographic voice—**Passion** and **Curiosity**.

Yo-Yo Ma said, "Passion is one great force that unleashes creativity, because if you're passionate about something, then you're more willing to take risks."

And French novelist Émile Zola wrote, "I prefer to die of passion than to die of boredom."

Walt Disney also had some words of wisdom: "When you're curious, you find lots of interesting things to do."

So my friend, my advice is also the **Mission** of this chapter, as follows.

YOUR MISSION
Work with Passion, Persistence, and Purpose—and stay curious.

3.
FINDING YOUR SUPERPOWERS & INNER VOICE

Batman doesn't have any superpowers. He has to use his brain and his courage. That's what always appealed to me.
— PATRICK LEAHY

L ike Batman, you have a superpower (or superpowers), but you may not know what it is at this moment. That's how I felt when I first started reading about superpowers.

I will share with you what I feel are my superpowers at the end of this chapter, but for now, let's first explore superpowers, and then how they relate to you and your photography and art—and to finding your inner voice.

What piqued my interest in the topic of superpowers, which probably goes back to the time of Plato and Socrates (and maybe before that, although likely known by a different description), was a conversation I had with my son Marco.

Knowing more than a few successful and talented people, I was saying to Marco that people who are good at one thing are usually good at many things. Marco began talking about why people are successful and mentioned superpowers, a new term for me at the time. I was fascinated and started surfing the web for information on superpowers.

My search brought me to an article by Konstantin Mitgutsch on medium.com. As Mr. Mitgutsch says in his article: "We have numerous hidden 'Superpowers' that are not just very human and personal, but really define who we are and could be on the deepest level. However, for a variety reasons, we've never understood this, let alone discovered these strengths and learned how to exploit them."

On forbes.com, Dede Henley argues that a superpower "isn't a skill but a perspective, a mindset, a way of working that enhances everything you touch."

To find our superpower, which defines our creative voice (among other things), we have to ask ourselves a few questions, taking photography out of the equation. The questions to ask are: What am I good at? What am I the best at? Why am I good at it? How did I get good at it? What do others think I am good at? Was I always good at it?

If all this talk about superpowers sounds far out (as we used to say in the 1960s), consider the following. After seeing a movie, you might say something like, "So and so is the best actor I've ever seen." Sure, the actor may be a terrific actor, but he or she drew on their superpower to excel in their craft. That may be the power to influence others through their facial expression, the tone in their voice, and their ability to convey strong emotions and feelings that they drew on from their past for their performance in the film.

Another example is the guitar work of Carlos Santana. Sure, he's a master guitar player, but his playing *perhaps* comes from his superpower, one of being very spiritual and mystical. You can read about his superpower on wsj.com in the article "The Mystical Journey of Carlos Santana." In effect, Santana is playing the same notes as a million other guitar players. But his superpower makes him unique and gives him his creative voice.

Relating this concept to photography, Ansel Adams, for example, used the same aperture and shutter speed as other photographers, but he was unique because he drew on his superpower or superpowers, which may have been an affinity for getting in touch with nature, and his ability to see contrast and envision the end result, using what he called "creative visualization."

In my quest to learn more about superpowers and our inner voice, I asked some of my well-known photographer friends about theirs. Take a look. Yes, these mentors are wonderful photographers, but their advice can be applied to many art forms.

SUSAN DIMOCK

Taking the time to "listen" to my own photography and process has been an important step for me in finding my voice. It has only been within the last couple of years that I have come to realize how my past career as a psychotherapist has influenced who I am in photography today. I did not fully understand this for a while, so at times I felt guilty for retiring early and "wasting" my degrees. Now I see nothing is for naught in life and everything we are and have been contributes to our voice as an artist.

As Ansel Adams said, "You don't make a photograph just with a camera. You bring to the act of photography all the pictures you have seen, the books you have read, the music you have heard, the people you have loved."

As a therapist, the art of listening is key to being successful. I believe speaking less and listening more can be useful on many levels in life, including in the realm photography. With that in mind, I'd like to suggest that this includes listening to ourselves more as well.

For me, this means tuning into my emotions and paying attention to my intuition. I find it interesting to have discovered that in my work as a photographer, it also includes listening with my eyes. In psychother-apy, of course, we would call this paying attention to body language.

Practically speaking, with my own photography, I discovered that listening to how I feel while shooting, as well as how I feel when I view my images, gives me important clues to pursue in the process of defin-ing my voice. This in turn, allows me to add depth and purpose in my work as a photographer.

A couple of years ago it started becoming very important to me to "find my voice." I needed to figure out why I'm taking photographs and what I want to do with them. I became weary of collecting images without purpose and wondered why I was continuing to shoot at all.

With that question in my mind, I began reviewing my portfolio and paying attention to how I felt as I did so. Amazingly, my own work began to reveal to me more about who I am as a person. Story lines began to show themselves and patterns and themes became apparent. I tuned into how I felt about these discoveries. I asked myself: What style and type of subject evoked emotion in me? What memories came to the foreground? What strengths and weaknesses did I notice? Where did I take risks? Did I sense any originality or uniqueness? What life lessons did I learn? Most importantly, what puts a smile on my face and causes me to linger? It is those two variables that indicate to me that I am moved by my own work and that I feel proud.

I apply these same concepts and questions to my process in the field. Am I enjoying myself? Do I feel exhilarated on a shoot or is it drudgery? Again, am I moved, and do I take time to linger and soak it all in? Once more, the answers, if we're honest with ourselves, are all vital clues as to how we can best move forward with an authentic and meaningful voice.

Naturally, there are many other things that are important as we move forward to define ourselves as artists. Things such as experiencing art within varied disciplines, traveling, reading, and going to museums.

All of these enrich our worldview and thus reveal themselves in our body of work. Rick speaks to a lot of these things in his book *Photo Therapy*

Motivation and Wisdom. And his voice is clear and meaningful.

To sum up, don't forget to look for clues and listen to your own work and process as well. Check it out, you may be pleasantly surprised at who you have become as a photographer, and as a person.

Through this introspective process of defining my personal voice and vision, I continue to learn about myself and what's important to me—and how I may contribute to this world.

Photography is a powerful medium through which to view ourselves, humanity, and this beautiful earth.

Lou Jones

Once upon a time, photography was an "outlaw" profession. Now it is the purview of soccer moms and anyone with a cellphone. In either case, it remains a wondrous way to make a living. In essence you get paid to "see."

Despite its benefits (and onslaught of current practitioners), it is a very difficult career path. Photographers come and go.

I have been doing this for a long time. Perhaps my greatest "superpower" is survival. Although photography has never been static, it has undergone a myriad of dramatic changes in the last few years. In the course of all the turmoil, I have seen every aspect of its evolution: equipment, large-format cameras with bellows and black cloth, Polaroid, film to digital, copyright, finances, privacy laws, computers, etc.

But survival skills are not glamorous superpowers. They are not sexy, like flying, x-ray vision, or an invisibility cloak. To weather these changes takes iron will, incredible persistence, and even mighty stubbornness.

A few of the fundamentals remain pertinent, but styles, technology, lighting techniques, postproduction, and delivery methods have so transitioned that successful photographers have to reinvent themselves periodically just to keep up.

From the beginning of its invention, photography has consistently increased its position in the pantheon of information, news, popular culture, and fine art. It is the essential building block of communications worldwide. It is so much a part of the fabric of day-to-day activity that it is impossible to chart its ascendancy.

Besides the mechanics and practices, perhaps aesthetics are the most difficult to fathom consistently. Morals pivot, opinions migrate, what is popular, or fashionable, undergoes revolution; the people who are curators and editors transition. As professionals, we have to recognize and adapt to the changes.

When I began this business, photojournalism was tantamount. Newspaper photographers were in abundance. Advertising and corporate/industrial photographers were major influences in the field. For a period of time, stock photography raised its formidable head. Now it is a shadow of its former self. Today the selfie and social media are where you see the most movement. But photography remains at the very epicenter.

For generations, the only "true art" was expressed in black-and-white, 8" x 10" prints. Now you cannot get noticed unless you are producing huge, color inkjet prints.

Ansel Adams's landscapes and Edward Weston's nautilus shells transmogrified into the murals of Chuck Close and Thomas Struth.

To be a chameleon and imitate the latest flavor-of-the-month can be career suicide, but to ignore the sea changes is to become irrelevant.

My degrees were in physics. I was once a rocket scientist. But to be a freelance photographer requires using all that I have learned. Besides the craft, I taught myself to be a lawyer, salesman, accountant, and enforcer. I manage a staff of assistants, direct models and production crews, and write books. None of these skills came naturally. They are not offered in school. It was a matter of necessity. Survival.

Photography is "skin in the game." It is the only art form where you *have* to be there. Herman Melville wrote *Moby Dick* having never set foot on a whaling ship. Pablo Picasso painted *Guernica* without going to war.

There is no road map or flight plan.

Photography is a competitive field with no handbook. And you cannot look it up online. The compliments of friends and family are of little help. They will love you no matter what and that false sense of security does not guide you through the minefields of commercial photography.

"Likes" on Instagram do not get you assignments. The pressure critics exert may have a negative effect on your personal vision. Ignore it all. Be resilient. You need to keep your own counsel.

Alone or relying on a small cadre of advisors, you find yourself out on the edge, susceptible to a lot of risk. Through experience, learn to trust your judgment, your talent, and your imagination. Get comfortable with insecurity. It stimulates your creativity. It is your best friend. Success breeds success.

Being a photographer is one of the greatest gifts imaginable. Independence. Depending on solving visual problems with your ingenuity rather than buying it makes you a real artist.

The superpower of survival may not get me noticed by Marvel or DC Comics, but as long as it allows me to make better pictures, attract new clients, and exhibit in galleries and museums, it certainly beats working for a living.

ALEX MORLEY

My superpower is attention to detail—almost to a fault, according to my wife.

It's in the pursuit of perfection. This is what has made me a good emergency physician over the years. I always try to not miss any detail— for the patient's safety and also to get the clues to figure out the diagnosis.

This translates to photography. Attention to detail is the superpower that keeps me in one place for hours waiting for that one element to happen. It's what keeps me going back to a location over and over to get the weather and light that will make a better image. It's striving for perfection. This never happens, but it's the pursuit of perfection and attention to detail that is my superpower.

GREG VAUGHN

I was having a hard time coming up with my superpower, so I asked my wife Penelope. She quickly responded: "Stepping back and assessing the entire situation before acting."

So how does this superpower relate to photography?

In my early years, I often acted impulsively, and when photographing, I would commonly start shooting as soon as I saw something of interest. That was not always a bad thing. I shot and then worked through a scene or situation to find the image.

These days, I'm more likely to analyze the scene and think about what is important, what I see, what I want to express, what I want to share, and how best to shoot/compose and process to get the message across.

Being able to step back and look at the overall situation also helps with personal relationships. Rather than react to a few words, I try to figure out what someone is really trying to express.

SCOTT BOURNE

My superpower is letting go.

As a bird photographer, I learn all that I can about the natural factors behind each photographic opportunity, but I never know how they will play out. My artistry focuses on the beauty of things that are random. Avian subjects operate within their own free will, on their own time and according to millions of years of genetic imprinting. In short, the bird flies its own path, and it's highly unlikely that I can influence that path.

This is different than working in a photography studio where I have control over the set, the model, and the lights. As a photographer who makes avian art, my power is knowing how to give up. I just show up prepared to interact with beauty that I don't control. I must learn to be at peace with my subject on their terms, not on mine. In other words, the only way to be successful is for me to give up all control. The peacefulness of that perfect space has infinite worth.

Karen Hutton

I've always felt as though my superpower is an ability to bring an ethereal quality into physical form and make it practical. I've always had it, since having a vision when I was a kid that imprinted itself on my soul. It involved light, awe, and the undeniable ability they have to heal and transform everything in their path.

But what do you do with *that* when it comes in like a lightning bolt as both a basic truth and a blueprint for your life when you're eight years old? What I did was set out to find a way to live it.

As a result, I understand the ways in which we're hardwired to experience awe and how it comes in through frequencies of light (hello photography), but I also understand how our very survival depends upon living that as our reality.

I've figured out ways to show people how to find that within themselves, to unlock it, and learn to trust it over any other voice. I've taught many disciplines—speaking voice, dance, figure skating, and acting— but art and photography has been the clearest path for me. After all, our medium is light!

My friends tell me that my photographic superpower is creating magic, both in-camera and through post-processing. Creating and capturing awe and showing the world awe still exists. I hope that's true! It's certainly the imperative that my muse seems to sing out in my ear from the moment I wake up each morning.

I try to use my voice—both the artistic and physical ones—to ignite and inspire. It feels as though it's the most authentic way to live and the most in keeping with what feels like the most powerful directive I've ever received, back when I was a sprout.

Steve Brazill

My superpower is interpretation. I have always had the ability to understand things at a very basic level.

That could be a script, photograph, story, or other environmental situation as I communicate or teach the meaning, emotion, story, or intent to others. Sometimes that manifests itself as me interpreting a voiceover script, the way the writer intended it, on the first take. Other times it comes out as helping to teach someone a concept through the use of various analogies. In every case it allows me to drill down to the root of an issue and help others to better understand it.

RON CLIFFORD

I'd say my superpower is that I'm an Inspirologist! Yes, I made up that term for Rick's book. I have the ability to help others see their creativity, even when perhaps they don't even see it fully themselves. I help others identify their unique strengths and then through thoughtful mentoring, critique, presentation, and practice, help them reach new creative heights. If I could be bold, I would dare say I help others reach their potential.

UNMESH DINDA

There are millions of people who are far better in Photoshop than I am, including my friend Rick Sammon, and I admire their work! The superpower that sets me apart is my love for teaching. No matter how complex the concept is, I somehow can break it down in a way that even a six-year-old can understand. Teaching has always been my gift; Photoshop is just a medium to practice my gift.

FRANK DOORHOF

People know me by my studio and fashion work, as well as my lighting techniques, but I feel my superpower is projecting my passion and joy onto my clients. And if I could offer some advice, I'd say try to project your passion, and the rest will follow.

SCOTT KELBY

Although I am mostly known as being skilled in Photoshop and Lightroom, and at making pictures, I think my superpower is teaching—

being able to communicate complex ideas in a simple and fun manner. I like to make learning fun.

PIPER MACKAY

My "authenticity" is what Rick calls a superpower. It's my deep passion and love for photographing the tribal people and wildlife throughout the African continent. I gave up everything to follow my photography dream, and now I am able—through my photography and my teaching—to inspire others to explore, respect, and try to preserve the beauty of our fragile planet.

JUAN PONS

My superpower is "getting in the zone," photographically speaking, when I have a subject of interest in front of me. I get completely immersed in observing and capturing my wildlife subjects and trying to make the best image I can—based on what I have researched about the species.

Getting in the zone photographically allows me to think like my subject, predict its behavior and position myself to make those great images. To me, this is the closest I get to a spiritual experience. It's like entering a meditative state.

KEN KAMINESKY

My superpower is "perseverance."

The photographic adventure has taken me on an evolutionary journey over the last thirty years, and it hasn't always been smooth sailing.

By learning to believe in myself, hard work, never giving up, and a sincere love of the craft, I'm now able to say that I'm exactly where I'm supposed to be, inspiring other people to fall in love with the world through the magic of their photography.

DON KOMARECHKA

My superpower is not caring if I'm right. I love to experiment, and I always have an idea in my mind of what I'd like to see, but I am thrilled with any outcome. Failures and mistakes should be reveled in, as you don't learn anything from doing it right the first time!

I might hypothesize that a photographic experiment will yield fantastic results, yet it turns out to be nothing more than a blurry mess; I embrace the challenge to learn from everything, sometimes enjoying the problem-solving process more than the results.

ART WOLFE

I think my superpower is the ability to entertain, educate and inspire. Sure, I love making photographs and writing books and doing television programs, but it's the thought of inspiring other that gets me out of bed in the morning. Sometimes I feel like a photography missionary, or perhaps more accurately, a photo emissary.

JULIE LEE

I think my superpower is that I am a prolific photo doodler.

What is photo doodling? It's very much like a coffee shop napkin where one draws an easy subject in as many variations as possible. There is no pressure to create a masterpiece, but only to explore the many ways of expression and warm up my creativity.

I am generous with the number of times pressing the shutter button when doodling. Mistakes are guaranteed and there will be many images I don't care for. I "doodle" from every angle, experiment with light, make long exposures, create intentional camera movement, shoot out of focus, use large and small apertures, try horizontal and vertical orientations, move close up and far away, and use (and break) as many compositional rules as possible.

I move to another subject after making an image that strikes a pleasant chord and recreate it with the new expression. I apply this to as many different subjects as possible just to see what it will create.

The key here is to keep trying, allowing myself to make mistakes. I have nothing to prove to anyone. Repetition is a great form of practice and developing a creative workflow.

Try photo doodling. With time and experimentation, your audience will see your unique personality within the images you share.

SEAN BAGSHAW

One of my superpowers is having a positive and upbeat outlook. I tend not to allow doubt or drama to get me down and I don't take most things too seriously. I honestly enjoy life, even with all its problems and challenges, and that applies to photography as well.

Perhaps the most pleasure in photography comes when I am able to teach something I have learned or been taught by someone else. Sharing and interacting with others who have the same interests as me is amazing!

Having a positive outlook and seeing reasons for gratitude improves my life and I hope it gives others a little lift as well.

MY TURN

So what is my superpower? Well, after pondering the question for a while, I think I draw on different superpowers in different situations, which is something that probably applies to you, too.

In my photography, it is the ability to communicate and have an awareness of the situation.

Because I love photographing "strangers in strange lands," communicating with the subject, most of the time without words, is the key to getting a good picture. Awareness plays into that, as I must be aware of everything that is going on around me, as well as being aware of how my facial expression, body language, tone of voice, and so on, is affecting the subject.

Being aware ties into another superpower that photographers, especially sports and wildlife photographers, need: it's the ability to see into the future, like a fortuneteller.

In other words, photographers need to be able to anticipate where and when a special moment will take place, and how light and shadows and color, as well as a subject's changing gesture, will affect a scene.

This fortuneteller superpower comes from experience, and I have drawn on my lifetime experience of taking pictures to be in the right place at the right time for many of my favorite photographs.

Communicating and awareness are also important in writing. Writers must communicate with their audience and be aware of their feelings. Writing is not a one-way conservation...if you "listen" to what the audience may say and think about how they will react.

I think my other superpower is an internal force that drives me to focus on a project and to never give up. That goes for writing a book with almost 45,000 words or installing a split-rail fence in my backyard (which was actually a ton of fun).

Take some time, from time to time, and try to identify *your* superpower. Once you find it and realize the effect it has on your photography (and life), my guess is that your photographs will have more meaning to you and give you a greater sense of satisfaction. You will feel empowered, like a comic book superhero, to leap to new photographic heights.

Another idea is to ask a loved one or friend what they think your superpower may be.

I recently asked a psychologist (who I was seeing in the 1980s and with whom I have kept in touch because he helped to cure me from crippling back pain) what he thought my superpower is. He answered: "I would say your superpower is some combination of your charisma and your boundless curiosity. I'm on the same page as your other psychologist friend who observed you don't want to miss anything in life, except I formulated the same observation in terms of your curiosity and sense of wonderment."

I opened this chapter with a quote about Batman, so I thought I'd end with a quote *from* this superhero, a quote with the message of encouragement: "You only have your thoughts and dreams ahead of you. You are someone. You mean something."

YOUR MISSION

Discover your superpower and be aware of its power in your photography and in your everyday life.

4.

YOUR SECRET WEAPON

I win in every fight; my secret weapons
are my kindness and forgiveness.
—DEBASISH MRIDAH

I n the preceding chapter, I encouraged you to explore your super-powers and special talents—all of them.

In this chapter, even though I have never met most of you, I can tell you that I know you have a secret weapon of sorts. It's something special that separates you from the crowd and makes you unique. This secret weapon will draw potential photography and art buyers to your site, participants to your workshops, encourage photographers/artists to attend your seminars, and bring subscribers to your blog and followers to your social media sites. It may also get you a job as a photo coach or art mentor on an exotic trip somewhere in the world.

This secret weapon is your personality.

I did not want to spill the beans on your secret weapon by using a quote to open this chapter, but I'll share two now: "Personality is everything in art and in poetry." —Johann Wolfgang von Goethe.

Here's another quote on one's personality: "Technique is really personality. That is the reason why the artist cannot teach it, why the pupil cannot learn it, and why the aesthetic critic can understand it." —Oscar Wilde.

My guess is that you, like most photographer readers of this book, know about the exposure triangle, how lenses affect a scene, how accessories can be used to enhance a scene, and how to use Photoshop and Lightroom to bring out the best in a digital file. In other words, you all know much of the same stuff.

It's *how* you share that stuff/information (through your personality), not *what* you share (by giving facts), that makes you unique.

As William Shakespeare said, "All the world's a stage, and all the men and women merely players; they have their exits and their entrances, and one man in his time plays many parts, his acts being seven ages."

I share Shakespeare's quote because, like actors working on their parts, we can work on our personalities, while still being ourselves.

In other words, we need to put our best foot forward—to have emotional intelligence and to be aware of how someone will react to us—and to know our effect on others.

For sure, when I am onstage or on-camera talking about photography (or on-camera talking about music, as I do on the Rick's Music Room section on my website), I "turn it on" and have more enthusiasm (which is contagious, by the way) then when I am playing guitar or keyboards in my music room all by myself. In a way, I am acting, but still drawing on the parts of my personality that I think people will like.

The same holds true for my writing. Although I try to write like I talk, I try to infuse more enthusiasm into my words than when I am "writing" my books in my head on my daily walks.

You don't, however, want to "turn it on" too much. For example, a TV pitchman with a fake smile, false enthusiasm, extra loud voice, and exaggerated body language who is promoting a product is often perceived (by smart/informed shoppers) as being obnoxious and as a fake. My friend, photographer, podcaster, and radio host Steve Brazill refers to this type of behavior, in radio terms, as "puking."

I refer to it as, "It looks like he's on drugs" (which was actually the case with boisterous TV pitchman Billy Mays, whose death at age fifty was caused, in part, by an overuse of cocaine, which can give one boundless energy).

If you need some guidance on projecting your true personality, I recommend taking the Dale Carnegie course on Effective Communications and Human Relations (as I recommended in **Chapter 2: What's Needed on the Photo Artist's Palette?**).

You can also practice your "act," so to speak, in front of friends and loved ones.

But always remember, as my Mother used to say, "To thine own self be true," which happens to be another Shakespeare quote (from his play *Hamlet*).

YOUR MISSION

Be aware of your secret weapon at all times, especially when speaking in public and when writing on public forums.

5.

THE ROLLERCOASTER
RIDE OF CREATIVES

Even a true artist does not always produce art.
— CARROLL O'CONNOR

When I speak to artistic photographers, those who are truly passionate about their work, I often begin by talking about the rollercoaster ride of all creatives. I say that on a rollercoaster the highs are high, and the lows are low, but that rollercoaster ride is much more interesting than being on a merry-go-round.

In other words, being a creative photographer, painter, and so on, is more exciting than being at a routine job that one does not like and that is not rewarding.

Here's my own rollercoaster ride story, one of them anyway: In the mid-1970s, I was just getting started with photography, and having some success in getting my pictures published in photography magazines. Back then, to get published, you needed to send query letters to editors. Well, one day I received one too many "No, thank you" letters.

Feeling low, I took down all the photographs on our living room wall and placed them around the garbage cans in the basement of our apartment building. I called the area my "Garbage Gallery."

I felt down for a while, but eventually got out of my funk when I received a letter saying that *LENS Magazine* wanted to run an article with my Hong Kong photographs and that the editor wanted to use one of my pictures on the cover.

Over the years, I have had many creative ups and downs, some of which caused crippling back pain, from which I have been cured for more than thirty years thanks to Dr. John E. Sarno and his teachings.

Riding the highs is a wonderful experience, but how do we pull ourselves out of the lows? Here are some suggestions, some of which apply to more than only photographers. Also note that these suggestions are good to keep in mind when you are riding the highs, too.

Know That You Are Not Alone on the Rollercoaster

Hey, I have been at this for a while. I have met hundreds of photographers who wanted to give up, one after he was told by a well-established pro to "sell his cameras." When that photographer came to me in despair, I told him that he was not alone, and to keep at it and to believe in himself. Today, that pro is leading photo workshops in India. I'm proud of him because he did not give up.

If you go on a photo workshop, you likely will meet people who, if they are honest, will tell you that at one point or another they felt down and alone. Remember, we are all in this together, and that includes me.

Take a Lesson

Feeling down about your photography or art? Take a lesson on something you have never tried before: golf, piano, guitar, singing, and so on. After your first lesson, which will be a humbling experience, my guess is that you will feel better about your photography...because you are probably better than you think you are.

Writer Josh Kaufman, author of *The First 20 Hours: How to Learn Anything Fast*, agrees with me when it comes to the "you are probably better than you think you are" philosophy. In his wonderful book, the author talks about the four steps needed to get good at something in twenty hours (as opposed to Malcolm Gladwell's "10,000 hours" philosophy that he outlines in his best-selling book, *Outliers: The Story of Success*). Those four steps are:

1) Break down a skill into its components.
2) Learn enough to know when you're making a mistake.
3) Remove any and all barriers to practice.
4) Practice for at least 20 hours.

So, my suggestion is: read both books. I am sure that after digesting the information on those pages, you will have more confidence in pursuing new goals.

SET REALISTIC GOALS

As you may know, one of my favorite adages is: "It's never too late to be what you might have been." Well, personally speaking, it's too late for me to be able to play guitar like Eric Clapton, Armik, or Carlos Santana. However, after some practice, I did learn some bass lines to some of their songs. Now I can actually play along fairly well when I listen to their songs on YouTube.

I set a realistic goal, not one that I knew was virtually impossible to reach. So, when setting a goal, be realistic.

TAKE A MASTERCLASS (MASTERCLASS.COM)

You'll find several photography classes on the MasterClass website where you can delve into the art and craft of photography. However, try taking a class on a different subject. That's a good idea because, I feel, what you learn in one area of creativity (and in life), you can apply to others. An example: Martin Scorsese's class on filmmaking will give you some excellent ideas on storytelling, which is what we do with our photography.

WATCH *CITIZEN KANE*

Orson Welles's 1941 movie, *Citizen Kane*, is a wonderful source of inspiration for, among other reasons, Welles's use of black-and-white photography and shadows and highlights. If you watch this movie with your one goal being to observe the photography, you may look at your photography in a new light.

Of course, there are other examples of movies that can inspire us with their creative image making, including *The Fountainhead* and *Sunset Boulevard*.

After watching one of these movies, try a new lighting technique or a new photo processing technique, perhaps on a photograph that you thought was "finished."

EAT HEALTHY

A healthy diet can improve our sense of well-being, as well as give us more energy. Plus, when we eat healthy, we feel better about ourselves. Remember, nothing tastes as good as skinny feels.

Speaking of eating, did you know that dark chocolate has plenty of health benefits, including easing emotional stress, according to a 2009 American Chemical Society trial? So it's okay to grab a bar of dark chocolate when you are down. Just make sure it's a mini-size bar.

GO FOR A WALK

We live in such a hectic world, always checking email, text messages, and so on, that it could drive one nuts. Take a break and take a walk. Refresh your brain. It's good for you. And keep this quote from Raymond Inmon in mind: "If you are seeking creative ideas, go out walking. Angels whisper to a man when he goes for a walk."

PLAY WITH PLUG-INS

Plug-ins for Photoshop and Lightroom, and stand-alone creative imaging programs can help us awaken the artist within.

Topaz Impression from Topaz Labs, for example, can transform a straight shot into an image that looks like a painting by Monet, Van Gough, Rembrandt, and other masters of the canvass.

Nik Collection Silver Efex Pro by DxO has presets, which you can fine-tune to create dramatic back-and-white images of which a seasoned pro would be proud.

Try an Artistic App

Smartphone photo apps are truly amazing, and some are capable of turning a snapshot into an art shot. I've done this with Distressed FX and Snapseed.

If you are feeling down, or just want to have some fun creating artistic images in the palm of your hand, try an app. I can tell you that I am a big fan of these apps, which sometimes surprise me with a very artistic end result.

Steal Like an Artist

Salvador Dalí said: "Those who do not want to imitate anything, produce nothing." I first learned of that quote in the book *Steal Like an Artist* by Austin Kleon. If you have "photographer's block," which is like writer's block to a writer, look up the work of a famous artist and try to copy/steal it. Writers with writer's block have a similar solution: they sit at the keyboard and type the words of a favorite novel.

Share

Sharing your work, and ideas, on social media sites is a good way to get inspired. If other photographers like your work, you'll get inspired by their comments, which will inspire you to make more creative pictures—and to post more pictures. Even if you are an established pro, feedback is important. I know.

Change

"When you are through changing, you are through." —Bruce Barton.

Change is good—and inspiring and refreshing. If change is good enough for a crawling sack of goo that transforms itself into one of the most beautiful creatures on the planet, then we should give it a try.

If you are stuck in a rut, get some inspiration by trying a different type of photography or by experimenting with different digital darkroom techniques. Challenge yourself. If you meet and exceed that challenge, you'll be inspired and motivated to try new things.

If you think you can't change, think about this adage: If you think you can, you can. If you think you can't, you can't. Have enthusiasm for all that you do—new and old—and inspire others, which is a good way for you to get inspired.

Remember: "Nothing great was ever accomplished without enthusiasm." —Ralph Waldo Emerson.

READ THE CHAPTER, "WHAT DOES YOUR PHOTOGRAPHY MEAN TO YOU?"

From my previous book, *Photo Therapy Motivation and Wisdom*. There you will find that you are not alone when it comes to feeling the importance of photography in your life.

READ MY FRIEND CHRIS ORWIG'S INSPIRING BOOK, *THE CREATIVE FIGHT: CREATE YOUR BEST WORK AND LIVE THE LIFE YOU IMAGINE*

Here's how Chris describes this important book: "Creativity is not a gift for a select few, but an ongoing process of growth and self-realization available to anyone who puts in the effort to pursue the spark. In this book, I try to offer a unique perspective on the creative process, showing you how to find meaning in your work, be inspired, and discover the life for which you were designed."

TAKE MY FRIEND ERIN BABNIK'S ADVICE

When you are feeling down, and stuck, and in a rut, "think more input than output." In other words, rather than taking pictures for the sake of taking pictures, see inspiration by going to museums, studying art and the work of other photographers, and so on.

TAKE CARLOS SANTANA'S ADVICE
Most people look for greatness in others. Take a moment and look inside. You may be surprised at who you meet.

MAKE A VISION BOARD
While you are on the rollercoaster, there is something very useful that can keep you focused and inspired: a vision board.

A vision board can be a large corkboard on which you tack goals, in the form of photographs, pictures of paintings, notes, and quotes. It could also be a magnetic board on which you attach items with magnets, or even a whiteboard on which you scribble ideas.

Yes, there are digital vision boards, but they require you to turn on your computer or iPad, a process during which it's tempting to check email and social media posts. So, I recommend going "old school" so you can have easy and readily available access to your vision board—your creative artistic and photographic goals.

Here are some examples of what one might put on a vision board, and why:

1) Inspirational quotes, such as: "It's always too early to quit." —Norman Vincent Peale. When you feel like giving up, this quote may inspire you to keep going.

2) Photographs of locations in which you'd like to photograph, say Antarctica or Africa. Look at the photographs and ask yourself how you can get there, maybe by leading a photo workshop, working with a tour operator, or getting an assignment.

3) A printed screen grab of a famous painting, such as Vermeer's *Girl with a Pearl Earring* or Renoir's *Girl Combing Her Hair*.

In your home, try to recreate the painting with a photograph. I did this with both paintings, and it was a creative and inspiring project, not to mention a ton of fun.

4) Stuff that has nothing to do with photography, such as screen grabs of CD covers that inspire you.

5) A photo that makes you smile or makes you happy, such as a funny photo or a photo of a lost loved one who added to your life. If you need a smile suggestion, print out a screen grab of Groucho Marx with his most well-known quote: "If you are not having fun, you are doing something wrong."

6) Print out these words and stick them on the board: Make someone happy today.

TAKE NOTES

Keep a note pad or your phone with voice messages handy, especially when you go to sleep or take a nap. I have found that I get many of my ideas while I am lying down and relaxing.

Ideas also come to me in the middle of the night.

When I get an idea, I get up and write it down. Sometimes, when I get up in the morning and read the scribbles on the piece of paper, I am surprised at what I've written. I might not have remembered the idea had I not written it down.

If you are serious about note taking, buy a nice, perhaps leather-bound, journal and maybe write more neatly. Keep this journal in a safe place. It may be more valuable than you think in years to come.

Part of the rollercoaster ride is going through phases, different periods of your creative life where you change your style, voice, and vision. Most often this is a good thing because as we change, we can grow. Or as Bruce Barton says, "When you are through changing, you are through."

I have gone through several phases, including my HDR phase in the mid-1990s. When I look at some of those HDR images, I ask myself, "What was I thinking?" I am glad I outgrew that phase, although at the time it seemed like the right thing to do.

Before my HDR phase, I went through an underwater photography phase, producing seven underwater photography books and scuba diving all over the world. That phase lasted twenty years. I stopped because I did not need another photo of a clownfish or a whale shark.

Musicians go through phases, too. Joni Mitchell, for example, began her career as a folk singer and eventually entered her jazz phase, which did not please some of her audience. But that did not matter to the singer/songwriter. She followed her heart and continued making the kind of music she wanted to make.

Painters go through phases, too. Picasso, for example, went through several phases, including his Blue Period (1903 to 1905), during which he painted sad and gloomy-looking people, using mostly a melancholy blue paint; and his Cubism Period (1907 to 1925), during which he transformed natural shapes into geometric forms on canvas.

The Three Musicians, a poster of the painting that I have hanging the wall in the room in which I am writing this book, is one such example of his cubism work.

So, phases are a part of the photographer's and the artist's life. They are part of growth. Being aware of these phases helps us on our photo quest.

Think about the phases you have gone through to get to this creative point in your life. Write them down. Look at them from time to time. Maybe even plan the next phase—chapter—in your photo quest.

YOUR MISSION
When you are feeling down, think about Norman Vincent Peale's motto: "It's always too early to quit."

6.

IDEA TO IMAGE

*Ideas are like rabbits. You get a couple and learn how to
handle them, and pretty soon you have a dozen.*
—JOHN STEINBECK

Every artistic creation—in photography, music, painting, writing, and so on—starts with an idea. Often, an idea goes through several incarnations before it becomes a reality. Of course, sometimes we realize that our original idea was not that great to begin with, so we ditch it, or maybe our original idea takes on an unexpected and even better reality. This is part of our photo quest.

When it comes to digital photography image-making, which starts with image capture and ends in the digital darkroom, on the web. or with a print, the idea-to-image possibilities are virtually endless. The only limitations are one's ideas, as well as not knowing all the possibilities of digital imaging programs. In reading these ideas, consider how they apply to painting, music, and other art forms.

Let's take a look at what I call the **Five Stages of the "Idea to Image" Process:**

1) IDEA—We get an idea for a photograph. Who knows from where it comes? Kurt Vonnegut, in one of his many books, suggests that ideas come from a chip implanted in our brain by alien beings.

Another source of ideas perhaps might be "God's thoughts," as Albert Einstein told his assistant and biographer Banesh Hoffman after he developed the Theory of Special Relatively.

Psychiatrist Carl Jung introduced us to the term "collective unconscious" in 1916. He felt our unconscious mind shares many similar thoughts and ideas of universal symbols and shapes, such as mothers, trees of life and the mystery of shadows, heaven, hell, and so on. So ideas may come from our unconscious mind.

LSD and other mind-altering drugs have also been known to generate unique ideas. (I am not recommending them here!)

We may also get ideas from drawing on images or subjects we have seen. Observing techniques we have seen—such as using depth-of-field or separation of subjects in a scene to tell our story—might be another source.

In many cases, we photograph what we recognize. For example, we may compose a landscape photograph drawing on our experience of looking at well-composed landscape photographs. If we see the shape of a head or the body of a naked woman in a rocky wall or on a sand dune, we may capture that area of the wall or dune (as I have done in both instances) as opposed to photographing a different area.

These types of human-form images are called anthropomorphic images. If we take a picture of a piece of floating ice that looks like a bird or other animal, that's called a zoomorphic image.

We also try to "copy" lighting techniques when it comes to landscapes, as well as portraits.

Abstracts, such as close-ups of rust and peeling paint, may have more of an original look, but even with abstracts, we try to see something that we recognize. This probably goes back to the caveman days when we, as humans, had to rely on our eyes for safety and food.

All of this is well and good. As Salvador Dalí said, "Those who do not want to imitate anything, produce nothing."

2) IMAGINATION—Our imagination is our unique gift that helps us

make images that stand out from the crowd of millions of pictures that are published every day on social media sites.

Before we even pick up a camera, we need to imagine how lighting, lens choice, camera settings, subject distance, and so on, will affect the image. We also need to imagine the possibilities that await us in the digital darkroom, especially when it comes to creative plug-ins. This is called pre-visualization.

One way to get good at imagining how a three-dimensional scene will be recorded as a two-dimensional image is to know your camera controls, your lighting setup, and to know Photoshop, Lightroom, and plug-in programs. The other way is to look at the work of other photographers and painters as often as possible.

3) EXPERIMENTATION—Dramatic lighting is an effective method for creating a unique image. When working with studio lights, experiment with moving the light an inch at a time. You will see how the shadows and highlights change on the subject's face. Also experiment with having the subject move his or her face to the left and right, and up and down, an inch at a time. Here, too, you will notice a difference in where the shadows and highlights fall.

When photographing a subject by window light, slight differences in subject position and the angle at which you are photographing make a difference.

In wildlife photography, experimentation is in the form of using wide or tight composition, capturing gesture, and looking for the art in nature.

In landscape photography, we experiment with depth-of-field, focus stacking, capturing light, and creative composition.

Of course, lots of experimentation takes place in the digital darkroom.

I'd like you to take a break from my text and do an online search for Miss Aniela (missaniela.com). Take a look, a good look, at her work. Then come back. Take my word. You will not be disappointed.

Miss Aniela's work is a wonderful example of the benefits of experimenting... as well as an example of using her imagination... as well as knowing her craft (in-camera capture and with Photoshop) as well as her creative visualization. I could go on, but you get the idea. Her work is a good example of the "idea to image" process.

4) IMAGE—After you have zeroed in on your idea, used your imagination, and have experimented, it's time to look into, not at, your picture.

Now it's time to ask yourself one or more of the following questions. Your answer or answers will help you find an answer to your main question: Is this a good image? The questions are:

+ Does the photograph have an impact? If so, how?
+ Is the photograph memorable? If so, why?
+ Does the photograph tell a story? In what way?
+ Does the photograph have a mood? What kind of mood?
+ Is the photograph original? In what way?
+ Will someone say my photograph is just a copy of another idea, and is that bad?
+ Would someone buy my photograph as fine art? Why?
+ Would a stock agency take my picture? For what genre?
+ Does my photograph hold a secret?
+ Does my image show a never-before-seen scene?

Another idea is to ask a family member or friend what they think of your photographs, and stipulate that you want them to be 100 percent honest, which is not easy for people when commenting on something so personal.

5) REVISITING—For some photographers, the "idea to image" quest stops with number four. For the serious *photo questers* (yes, I just made up that term), a photograph is never really finished. They go back again

and again and reprocess an image using new ideas and/or new features in Photoshop and Lightroom, the latter being similar to re-mastering an old recording of The Beatles so the recording sounds better, clearer, and fuller.

Speaking of The Beatles and re-mastering, Ringo Starr (the drummer of The Beatles, for the youngsters out there) said: "I love the remastered versions of the song because now you can hear the bass drum, because the bass sounds were the first to go on old recordings."

Another example: Ansel Adams said, "A photograph is never really finished." This master photographer and printer went back again and again to the wet darkroom to reprocess his images—to make the finest print he could make.

I think it's a good idea to revisit your images from time to time. You may be surprised at what you find, and learn, on your visit.

And speaking of visiting, "visit" Leonardo da Vinci's painting *St. Jerome in the Wilderness* online. Notice the depth and dimension of the painting. Leonardo revisited the painting twenty years after he "finished" it, applying new and different techniques to make the painting one of his finest masterpieces.

On the other hand, visit his *Ginevra de' Benci*. It's an older painting that he did not revisit. Compared to his *St. Jerome in the Wilderness* and *Mona Lisa* paintings, this painting looks flat.

Yes, all this stuff I just said about Leonardo is subjective.

Well, my friend, I hope you have fun with the "idea to image" concept and the process—and the rollercoaster ride—on your photo quest. As the Zen saying goes: Enjoy the process and the moment.

Hey, you don't need to be Zen monk or master to follow their philosophy. But please do keep in mind that these thoughtful individuals don't care about results; they focus on habits, rituals, and processes that support the Zen way of living.

Don't rush the "idea to image" process. This philosophy is summed up in a very important Zen saying: "Don't rush life. Before you know, it will all be over."

Remember, practice makes perfect. Don't worry about the length of time it takes you to reach your idea of perfection. As another saying goes: You can't spend too much time working on an image because your soul is in the image.

Here's a Zen short story that illustrates that it takes time to reach perfection. It's called, *The Old Man and Practice*.

One day, a boy playing on the beach saw an old man in the distance. The old man was in a squat position and seemed to be looking down at the ground.

As the boy moved closer, he saw that the old man was drawing a perfect circle into the sand.

"Hey, old man, how did you draw such a perfect circle?" the boy asked.

"I don't know, I just tried, and tried again. Here, you try," the old man replied as he slowly turned his head and looked at the boy.

The boy took the stick and the old man slowly walked away.

The boy, perplexed, began drawing circles in the sand. At first, his circles came out too wide, or too long, or too crooked. But as time went by, the circles began to look better and better.

The boy kept trying and trying, and then, one bright morning, he drew a perfect circle into the sand.

Then he heard a small voice behind him.

"Hey old man, how did you draw such a perfect circle?"

Here's another Zen short story about how perfection means different things to different people.

One day an old monk informed a priest that important guests were expected. Immediately, the priest began tending his garden. He removed weeds, pruned tree branches and shrubs. He even combed the moss. Because it was autumn, the ground was untidy with dry leaves that the priest painstakingly raked and arranged into neat mounds.

All this time, the old monk was watching him from the other side of a wall. The priest finished with his labor of love. A look of satisfaction spread across his face. *"Doesn't it look beautiful now?"* he said, turning to the old monk.

"Indeed, it does," replied the old monk, *"but something's not quite right. Here, give me a hand over this wall and I'll fix it for you."*

Puzzled, the priest did as he was asked. The old monk made his way slowly to a tree in the center of the garden, gripped its trunk and shook it very hard. Leaves—orange, russet, and brown—fell to the ground. *"There, that's better. Now, please help me back across the wall."*

YOUR MISSION
Enjoy the process and remember to "shake the tree" every once in a while.

7.

THE IMPORTANCE OF YOUR CONVERSATION

"Life is a conversation. Make it a good one."
—GLENNON DOYLE MELTON

I was lucky to see Carlos Santana perform at Woodstock in 1969. Back then Santana was an innovative musician. Today, he is still an amazing composer and performer, but he is also a wonderful teacher, offering one of my favorite online MasterClasses (masterclass.com), *The Art and Soul of Guitar*.

In the two-minute promo for the class, Santana talks about what one will learn in the class. As I was listening, I could relate each of his topics to photography.

Let's explore those topics and how they relate to our photo quest process. Even if you are not a musician, I think you will be able to relate to this analogy.

MUSIC STRINGS THE MIND TO THE HEART—IT'S A CONVERSATION

The best thing I learned from the class is Santana's philosophy about how playing the guitar should be like having a conversation with the audience. He is "talking" to the audience with his music.

We can say the same thing about our photographs. They should "speak" to the audience, have a message or an emotion or a feeling, be it a landscape or wildlife photograph, or a portrait.

One way to determine if a photograph has something to say is to write a caption for it. If you can't write a caption, maybe the photograph has no message.

That said, Beethoven wrote *Moonlight Sonata* (a beautiful title), which had something beautiful to say, as well as Sonata Opus 106 (a relatively boring title), which also had something beautiful to say. My point is that if you can't write a caption, the photograph may still speak for itself.

MUSIC BRINGS LIGHT INTO THE DARKNESS

What Santana means is that music can light up the soul, bring happiness into one's life, and chase away fear.

Photography can do the same thing when everything—an interesting subject, good in-camera exposure, and thoughtful processing—comes together to produce a photograph that evokes a conversation with the viewer.

MUSIC HELPS MUSICIANS UNFOLD THEIR WINGS

Like music, photography can help one grow not only as an artist, but also as a person because as we learn, we grow, and learning, as the Buddhists say, is health.

Photography has not only given me wings, having had the good fortune to travel to more than one hundred countries, but it has allowed me to learn about different cultures and what's important to them. So, for me, photography is not about the exposure triangle, it's about having a conversation with the subject.

As you search for your photographic and creative voice, take note of your flight to your goal. Your wings will grow stronger if you *never give up* and photograph with passion, purpose, and persistence.

On your creative flight, you may set your sights high—on the stars in the sky. It's good to aim high. However, if you don't reach that goal and only hit the moon, I think you are doing all right.

MUSIC GIVES PEOPLE A REFERENCE TO AN ATTITUDE

Here's one of Santana's explanations about this. He says that before his band arrived in San Francisco in the mid-1960s, the girls would dance with their hands flowing slowly and gracefully above their heads, as if they were catching butterflies. He goes on to say that when his band played, the girls would dance as if they were saying, "Come and get me."

Through his innovative music, which conveyed the feeling of passion and strength, Santana was able to stir emotions with his audience.

Photographs—your photographs—can have a similar effect on people. One of your beautiful landscape photographs can bring happiness to someone. A photograph of a dearly departed loved one may make a relative or friend cry. An extreme close-up of a flower may make someone appreciate the wonders of Mother Nature. And of course, photographs taken of man's inhumanity to man can make us angry and sad.

You can see an example of the power of a picture by doing a web search for "30 of the Most Powerful Images Ever." As you will see, the photographs speak to the viewer, starting a conversation.

In some cases, a conversation started by a photograph can have a profound effect, as was the case of the photograph taken in Vietnam during the Vietnam War of a little girl running naked, her clothes having been burned off, toward the photographer. This single photograph—*The Napalm Girl*, taken by Nick Ut—started the conservation that eventually helped to end the war. It changed, as Santana would say, people's attitude.

MUSIC GETS PEOPLE'S ATTENTION

Music is an attention-getter for sure, but so is a photograph. Walk through any major international airport and your attention is grabbed—through the use of top models, exquisite makeup and styling, and dramatic lighting—by the large ads for fashion and beauty products.

Magazine editors select cover photographs based on their attention-getting qualities. Many factors go into such an image, including the subject, lighting, color, feeling, and emotion. When you are taking a picture, one question to ask yourself is: Will it be an attention-grabber?

Think about the picture hanging on the wall of an art gallery, or the wall of a local coffeehouse. When someone walks by, will they stop and take a closer look? If so, why? If not, why not? The answers will help you take a closer look at your photograph.

Getting back to my guitar hero, Santana goes on to say that he is often asked: "What kind of pedal are you using? What kind of strings are you using on your guitar? What kind of guitar and amp do you use?"

He says, "It's not about the gear. It's about connecting the soul with the mind and body."

If we are passionate about our photography, the same philosophy holds when it comes to our photographs.

A photograph is not only about a connection and conversation between you and the subject in the frame, but it's about a connection between the viewer of your photograph and the subject in your photograph.

When it comes to viewing a photograph, psychology plays a very important role (as an advertising creative director, fine-art photographer, or painter will tell you). These skilled craftsmen know a photograph is viewed in one of three ways: 1) we project our feelings onto the subject, 2) we hear a subject "speak," or 3) we become one with the subject.

Let's expand on those thoughts.

PROJECTING FEELING

It is natural for us to project our feelings onto a subject, not only when it comes to photography and art, but also with any aspect of life, especially when it comes to love.

Projecting our feelings onto a subject is the case when it comes to anthropomorphism, the process by which we imagine animals, or other non-human subjects, exhibiting human feelings.

SPEAKING SUBJECTS

This technique is about looking at a subject and letting it "speak" to us about its individuality, as far out as that may sound to some. When I taught a workshop in California with John Sexton, one of Ansel Adams's assistants, John talked about listening to trees, of which he has made many photographs that literally "speak for themselves."

BECOMING ONE

"Become one with the force" is the Jedi warrior's creed in the *Star Wars* movie series. My golf instructor tells me I need to "become one" with my golf club. And in the "Wedding Song" by Peter, Paul, and Mary, they sing, "the two should be as one."

In photography and in art, another method to connect with the subject is to become one with it. We can accomplish that goal by learning about a subject before we set off to photograph it. We can also develop a connection by simply looking at a subject for a long time and wanting to be close to it.

Indeed, a photograph, or painting, or sketch is viewed in one of three ways. While that is true, you can also look at a single photograph in all of the three ways, but at different times.

The more you think about the three basic ways in which a photograph is viewed, the more closely you will look at the scenes in your camera's viewfinder, your photographs, as well as the photographs of others.

If all this psychology stuff sounds too far out, think about the popular adage (often misattributed to Sigmund Freud) that sometimes, a cigar is just a cigar.

That said, when you see a subject that you want to capture, it's a good idea to ask yourself: "Why do I want to take that picture?" The reason or reasons may be very revealing.

Getting back to the title of this chapter, "The Importance of Your Conversation," there is a very important aspect of conversation that we need to keep in mind: listening. As Dale Carnegie points out in his book *How to Win Friends and Influence People*, listening is the key to having a good conversation.

I'll talk more about listening in **Chapter 14: Know Your Audience & Build Your Brand**. But, for now, I recommend reading Dale Carnegie's book, which was written in 1936, and taking the Dale Carnegie course, Effective Communications and Human Relations, which I took in 1985. This course helped me tremendously in many aspects of my life, from interacting with people in foreign countries to working on the business side of my career. My wife Susan agrees. We are both proud graduates of the course.

YOUR MISSION
Always keep the "conversation" of your photographs in mind.

8.

CRITICISM: THE GOOD, THE BAD AND THE UGLY

Don't be distracted by criticism. Remember—the only taste of success some people have is when they take a bite out of you.
—ZIG ZIGLAR

"Any fool can criticize, condemn, and complain—and most fools do."
—DALE CARNEGIE.

When considering the opening quote for this chapter, I was torn between the one I used and this one:

Both quotes hit home and ring true when it comes to criticism, which is part of a deal for photographers and all artists these days on social media sites, and on Amazon.com for authors.

If I wanted to keep this chapter short, my best advice would be: have a tough skin, don't let negative comments get you down, and people are always throwing rocks at the person on the top of the pile. Or maybe even better advice would be to think about what my mother told me when I was young: "You can't make all of the people happy all the time and not everyone is going to like you."

However, criticism is such an important topic that I'd like to spend time exploring the positive and negatives effects of it. But first, I'd like to ask you a question: What's the best pizza place in your neighborhood? Think about the crust, sauce, cheese, topping, and so on. Have your answer?

Well, my guess is that if I asked twenty of your neighbors the same "best pizza" question, not everyone would agree with you. They may even criticize your favorite pizza as having too much olive oil or not enough cheese.

I think you get the idea. We all have different tastes—in photographs and, of course, in pizza!

In looking at criticism, it's important to ask oneself this all-important question: Why is someone criticizing me? Some possible answers:

+ The criticizer simply does not like your photography or work.
+ Subconsciously or consciously, the criticizer feels that you remind them of someone they don't like—a parent or even a part of themselves (although they may not realize the latter).
+ The criticizer is jealous of your accomplishments, lifestyle, and even your happiness.
+ Or the criticizer is a negative thinker.

When you consider these reasons, my guess is that you will feel better about your work and, more importantly, your life.

I have some experience dealing with negative comments about my work on Amazon.com, having written forty books before this one. I have seen and heard it all, from top to bottom.

In the beginning, I used to let bad book reviews (such as, "Look what the camel dragged in") get me down. By the way, that book, *The Complete Guide to Digital Photography 2.0*, had a photo on the cover of a camel on a sand dune silhouetted by a setting sun.

I still read my reviews, but now I take them with a grain of salt. Or, as one of my friends suggested, toss out all the 5-star and 1-star reviews and you'll see what honest people think.

When I hear negative comments, I consider my mother's words of wisdom. I also know that it's easier to criticize than to create and wonder what type of picture or body of work the criticizer would have created under similar circumstances.

Sometimes I respond to bad reviews. Here are two of those responses:

"It's easier to criticize somebody else than to see yourself."
—GEORGE HARRISON

"Successful people will always be attacked in some form or another, and usually by those that lacked the courage to reach for their dream or to make a difference in their lives or the lives of others."
—ANONYMOUS

What I don't do is get sucked into a rabbit hole by a troll, and there are many out there for sure. You never want to get emotional on the web.

My friend Trey Ratcliff, who runs the successful and awesome stuckincustoms.com website, had some not-so-nice reviews in 2009

when he published *A World in HDR*, which I found quite interesting and informative.

Not everyone felt the same way as I did. Here are three titles of my "favorite" negative reviews of that book: 1) HDR sucks, 2) huh?!?!, and 3) Wow, I have high dynamic resentment.

Trey handled the negative comments interestingly and creatively: he made a video recording of himself reading the reviews with a strong and exaggerated English accent. It was hysterical.

I think we all know deep down what we think is a good photograph, good photography book, or a good photo exhibit. So when you read the reviews on Amazon, Instagram, and other sites, look for advice that will help make you a better photographer, author, or artist. Don't let the naysayers get you down.

Let's take a closer look at the helpful and harmful, or positive and negative, ways to view criticisms. But first, if you want to avoid criticism, follow Elbert Hubbard's advice: "To escape criticism: Do nothing, say nothing, be nothing." In other words, rather than trying to make a great photograph, go bowling!

POSITIVE EFFECTS OF CRITICISM

+ It makes us take a closer look at our work and ourselves.
+ It may produce a new idea or a new take on an idea.
+ It might make us feel not full of ourselves.
+ It gives us a reason to try a new photographic or artistic idea.

All of these effects can help us in our photo quest—if we have a positive attitude and realize that, as a bumper sticker in the 1960s said, "I could be wrong."

NEGATIVE EFFECTS OF CRITICISM

+ It makes us angry.
+ It makes us sad.
+ It makes us want to give up.
+ It makes us overreact and do something stupid.

Here, too, when reading negative criticism, keep in mind the saying on the bumper sticker. The critic may have a valid point and you could be wrong. More importantly, however, try not to feel "down" and know that you are not alone when it comes to being criticized.

So far, we have talked about criticism from other people. There is another, sometimes even stronger critique: the one inside you. Often, we are our own strongest critics, which can be both helpful and harmful.

If you are a perfectionist, you know about your inner critic. And "thanks" to social media, that inner critic is more vocal than ever. Here, too, think about that bumper sticker.

So yes, you could be wrong about your work, and your work might be, and probably is, better than you think it is. Here are two examples, one short and one long:

1) I give online portfolio reviews. As the photographers who have taken the sessions will tell you, the first thing I say is: "You are a good photographer. Why have you come to me for advice?" I have shared that experience on several podcasts, as well.

2) I am a member of the KelbyOne community, which includes access to forums where members can share ideas, post comments, and ask for advice.

After seeing Scott Kelby give a talk during which he shared some awesome photographs, a member started a discussion with the title of the post being "Maybe it's time to give up." (If you are a KelbyOne member, you can find this discussion by typing that title in the Search window on the site.)

I was reminded of my own "Garbage Gallery" story that I talk about in **Chapter 5: The Rollercoaster Ride of Creatives.** Here's what I told the photographer:

"Hey! I have felt disappointed with my work from time to time. When I look at one of the chapters in my HDR book, I say to myself, what was I thinking?

"Maybe take a break. When I go away for two weeks and don't play guitar, I think I sound better when I come home. It's good to take a break.

"Comparing is not the best advice. Follow your heart and never give up. NEVER.

"The good news is that you are evaluating your work. We all must do that to grow.

"Also…all the positive comments here on the forum about your work speak for your work!"

Yes, there were lots of positive comments on the forum. Here are just a few:

+ I just went to your Instagram and WOW!!! What in the world are you talking about? Your images are fantastic!!!
+ Geez, I wish my snapshots looked so good.
+ I've been there. And visit "there" frequently. Two things help me. One is just taking a break; two, stop applying rules and just let your heart and eye guide you. And for me, just me, the artistry of an image often happens in Photoshop and just playing with it and trying stuff without thinking about what is good or correct.
+ The thing that helps me most is having feedback from fellow photographers, criticizing my pictures, in person, not through

social media—hence the constant improvement. Courses alone provide knowledge, but that's far from being enough.

- I went and looked at your Instagram feed. I think you are being way too hard on yourself! I love your pictures! Try a photo project to re-inspire yourself.
- I'm sure you're being too hard on you! You're probably comparing yourself to the best photographers in the world and feeling bad about it.

So my question to you, dear reader, is this: Have you been there, felt that way? See? You are not alone.

I'd like to follow up on the last comment about comparing. I know it's easy to say, and even I don't follow this advice all the time, but it's not healthy to compare, as did the "Maybe it's time to give up" photographer.

Here is just one reason why: You may not know all the help the photographer had in getting that great shot! For example, I have some pretty good white horse pictures in my "Carmargue Horses" gallery on my website. You might look at them and think, "Wow! Rick is a pretty good horse photographer." Well, first I'd say thank you, but then I'd tell you all the help I had in making those pictures. Here's that help list:

- French cowboys and cowgirls skillfully herded the horses into the picture position for a photograph.
- I worked with a local photographer, Patrice Aguilar, who knew the best locations for the shoots.
- Patrice also knew the best times of day to be in the locations.
- At each location, we did four or five runs to ensure that we all got the shots.

Yes, I got the shots, but I would not have gotten the shots if it had not been for all the help behind the scenes. So here's a related bit of advice: get all the help you can get, and always give credit, as I did above, where credit is due.

I mentioned, "I/you could be wrong" a few times in this chapter. As an artist, considering this option is very important, and it's summed up very eloquently in this quote:

"One of the great challenges in this world is to know enough about a subject to think you are right, but not enough about the subject to know you're wrong." —Neil deGrasse Tyson (American astrophysicist, author, and science communicator), from the promotion for his online Master Class teaching scientific thinking and communication.

I'd like to end this chapter with a short story about critics.

A young artist exhibits her work for the first time, and a well-known art critic attends her opening.

The critic says to the young artist, "Would you like to hear my opinion of your work?"

"Sure," the artist says.

"It's worthless, the critic says.

"I know," the artist replies, "but I want to hear it anyway."

YOUR MISSION
Try not to be too hard on yourself.

9.

FINE ART: PUBLIC OPINION AND POCKETBOOKS

"I don't care if you make a print on a bath mat,
as long as it's a good print."
—EDWARD WESTON

Of course famed fine-art photographer Edward Weston was not really suggesting that you make a print on a bath mat. What he was saying is that a print, first and foremost, must look good and have impact—and that the paper on which an image is printed comes second. It's kind of like the photography adage: Cameras don't take pictures, people do.

The topic of printing often comes up when discussing one's creative photo quest—not just printing for oneself, but printing for exhibits. In reading the following, you'll see how this applies to painters, as well.

For insight into this topic, I turned to my photographer friend Edward Cooley, who I met several years ago on photo workshop in Provence, France. Since then, Ed has moved into the world fine art photography and printing, and he has become an expert on the topic (he opened the Ed Cooley Gallery, where he sells his own photography, and Steam Art and Graphics, where his team makes exhibition-quality metal prints for other photographers and artists).

As fine art photography and printing is part of many a photographer's photo quest, I asked Ed to write a piece for this book. Take it away Ed, and thank you!

ED COOLEY

As photographers on a quest for artistic fulfillment, we often question the value of our work. There are moments of exhilarating joy when everything falls into place to realize our pre-visualization of the shot. The process of crafting that image into a finalized work of art can take hours or days.

How can others experience the emotional impact of artistic expression we personally enjoy as photographers? Is there value in our work beyond the personal experience of capturing that image and sharing it freely on social media?

We all follow the same path to some degree. We learn the basics of focus, exposure, and composition. After the basics come technical excellence, artistic vision, and finally, personal style. This takes years and should continue, as our quest is a journey that never ends.

Comparing our work from year to year, we should see consistent improvements. The beauty of artistic expression is that it continually evolves through time and experience. The more you learn to see, the more you'll have to say technically and artistically. Eventually you become confident enough in that vision to call yourself an artist with photography as your medium of choice.

At some point during this quest, there is a crossroad where we must decide if our work has merit beyond personal enjoyment or commercial work. Most importantly, this decision in scope and timing is yours alone. Not every photographer will pursue photography as a career, and even fewer as a career in the arts. Many will enjoy it as a personal hobby and create incredible, professional-quality images. An amateur career in photography should not, in any way, be considered a negative—all enjoyment without the frustration of earning a living.

Confidence in your creativity and artistic vision is important because the road to success in fine art is a long and difficult drive. If you are not sold on your work, the decision is already made—you're not quite ready.

Do you feel you are destined for a career in artistic photography? Craft and frame some large prints of your work and hang them prominently in your home. If the art is still interesting after a month or two, then that is good confirmation of potential value. Once you feel confident your work has appeal, you may be ready to make the leap and engage the marketplace.

Art has always been about the physical object, and the current day consumer values photographic prints to a greater degree than ever before. These prints are called "fine art" because the expectation is lasting value, and to a lesser extent, resale value. These finely crafted prints are sold in large sizes and small quantities, or "limited editions," which enhance the concept of value.

The industry refers to patrons as "collectors," which adds another dimension to the genre. These "collectors" don't just buy one piece, they follow you during your career, collecting pieces they admire along the way.

Value is determined less by the work and more by the artist. Collectors must be sold on you first, then they acquire your art that speaks to them. This doesn't mean you have to be "world famous" to earn a decent living in fine art. It does mean cultivating your artistic brand is just as important as the quality of your work.

During Art Basel Miami 2019, a limited-edition work by Maurizio Cattelan entitled "Comedian" sold for $120,000. In fact, the third and final edition sold for $150,000. That's a nice $390,000 payday for the artist and the gallery representing him.

I personally experienced the work and it was so dramatic that a line of spectators waited to take selfies with it. Perhaps you read about it, a fresh banana duct taped to the wall. You or I couldn't get a dollar for a photo of a banana duct taped to a wall. Cattelan, however, understands that the artist and his story determine value.

Public opinion about your work is not nearly as important as the value of your brand as a visual artist. Respect and promote your work as a statement of artistic vision. Engage the marketplace and you may become the next Maurizio Cattelan, Andreas Gursky, or dozens of other artists who have cultivated their personal brands into a respectable career.

EDWARD COOLEY
edcooleyfineart.com

Thank you again Ed for your insight into the world of fine art photography and printing.

On a related topic, my friend Alec Arons has this thought on printing:

The most powerful part of creating art is the ability to hold it in your hands. In the case of image making, you are not done until you make a print. I remember my first workshop where we each had the opportunity to print an image. As I held my photograph in my hands, I could not stop thinking, "I can't believe I made this."

I will admit now that all I did was push the shutter on a scene composed by others, but I saw the possibilities and became hooked. Now when I hand someone a print and I see their reaction; it gives me a burst of fuel to continue my photo quest.

I started this chapter with a well-known quote about printing. I'll finish with a well-known adage: If you can't make a good print, make a big print. Sure, it's a joke, and I have seen some pretty bad big prints.

YOUR MISSION
Set a goal of making a fine art photograph and a fine art print.

10.

SPECIALIZING OR NOT SPECIALIZING

Be faithful to that which exists nowhere but in yourself—and thus make yourself indispensable.
— ANDRÉ GIDE

O ne of the most important decisions an artist needs to make is to be a specialist or a non-specialist, because there are pros and cons to both.

I know photographers who specialize in landscape photography, sports photography, wildlife photography, close-up photography, studio photography, and so on.

Within a specialty, there can be a more specific specialty. My friends Jonathan and Angela Scott are one such example. They are wildlife photographers based in Kenya, but their real specialty is big cat (lion, cheetah, and leopard) photography. They are known as "The Big Cat People."

I also know photographers who, like me, don't specialize, although I jokingly say that my specialty is not specializing.

The same "specializing or not specializing" concept can be applied to other art forms. For example, guitarist Carlos Santana plays jazz, rock, and Latin music—and more.

My photographer friend Art Wolfe is a prime example. On location around the world, Art photographs wildlife, nature, landscapes, tribes, and more. In the studio, Art photographs what he calls "The Human Canvas," a project that resulted in a book of the same name, and which involved photographing artfully painted people posed against original hand-painted backgrounds. Yes, Art did all the painting, too.

Unlike a doctor who can give you good advice if they correctly diagnose a particular problem, I don't think a successful professional photographer/artist who specializes or does not specialize can give you advice as to which path to follow because both work, and they work for different types of people.

For me, not specializing works. I say to novice photographers that if you are good in one area of photography, you are probably good in others, even if you don't know it.

For example, if a photographer is good at close-up flower photography, they would probably be good at food photography, because several of the same principles apply—arrangement, shallow depth-of-field, and making an image with impact

For Ansel Adams, specializing in landscape photography worked. For Arthur Morris, specializing in bird photography paid off, big time. And for Karsh of Ottawa, specializing in studio portraiture was a very good decision.

Of course, over a lifetime, a photographer/artist can go back and forth between the two, which also works.

To give you some insight into which path to take, I thought I would share with you some quotes on specializing. After that, we'll take a look at what some of my friends say about which way to go.

First the quotes:

Nuno Roque: "I spent most of my life trying to specialize myself. I went to theatre school, film school, music school, mime school, art school…Finally, I was able to gather enough knowledge to build the confidence to create my own work, that goes utterly against the sense of specialization."

John Steinbeck: "Maybe, kneeling down to atoms, they're becoming atom-sized in their souls. Maybe a specialist is only a coward, afraid to look out of his little cage. And think what any specialist misses—the whole world over his fence."

Robert M. Pirsig: "The range of human knowledge today is so great that we're all specialists and the distance between specializations has become so great that anyone who seeks to wander freely between them almost has to forego closeness with the people around him."

Alexander Pope: "One science only will one genius fit."

Plato: "Each man is capable of doing one thing well. If he attempts several, he will fail to achieve distinction in any."

Now let's get some insight about specializing from three of my professional photographer friends. Here, too, think about how photography ideas can be applied to other art forms.

FRANK DOORHOF

When it comes to specializing or not specializing, I feel that for creative professions like photography, music, drawing, and so on, it's advisable *not* to specialize because what you learn in one area of photography can be applied to another, making you a better all-around photographer.

For example, believe it or not, knowing about landscape photography immensely helped me get better photographs of models on location because both types of photographs are about light, composition, and of course telling a story. Also, I don't have any feeling for architectural photography, but I still photograph an interesting building, knowing that with the knowledge I get from just playing around with angles, composition, etc., my photography, in general, will improve.

When you *do* want to specialize in a specific area of photography, determine what you love, which you can only find out by literally photographing every kind of subject for a while, and then by playing with the end results.

Rather quickly, you will find the "right stuff" that hits home for you. However, I suggest that you keep photographing a variety of subjects for the very simple reason that the *process* will help with your *progress* to become a better all-around photographer.

Now that you know you can *specialize* or *specialize by not specializing* (I stole that idea from Rick) you can determine which path to choose, which of course you can change, and change again and again, as you grow as a photographer.

And please keep this thought in mind: we only live once (I think), so my best advice is to specialize in loving what you do.

STEVE BRAZILL

Most photographers that I know specialize in some way. I know wedding photographers, landscape photographers, senior photographers, macro photographers, and the list goes on and on. Almost everyone specializes, or do they?

In many ways, wedding photographers are a variation of portrait photography, and the same goes for senior photographers. Most macro photographers are wildlife, nature, and/or landscape photographers, but on a very tiny scale.

I am a music photographer. That is pretty much all I do, all I want to do, and part of how I see myself. Like everyone, I will venture into a different genre now and then, but the truth is it's rarely something I am excited about. I get hired periodically as an event photographer, but I tend to avoid saying yes to those jobs.

Music has been a part of my life for as long as I can remember, and I have been in radio for over forty years. Music is what gets me up when I feel down or calms me when I'm upset or anxious. Music is in my blood.

To look at why I specialize in music photography, I need to go back in time, way back. Some of the best memories from my youth were looking at the photographs of the bands I loved and wishing I could be on that stage.

There was Led Zeppelin, Aerosmith, CSNY, Hendrix, The Doors, KISS, and so many more. Can you picture any of those? Can you see those pictures? The odds are many reading this can remember the same images I do. That is why I take photographs, and why I specialize in live music. I want to make images that define the music of a generation.

So what does specializing in music photography look like? I photograph concerts, and many things at a concert involve photography, starting with things that happen behind the scenes. Nowadays, bands sell VIP experiences that often include a meet & greet. That's where the fans get to meet the artist they love (for about two minutes) and get a photo with them, and someone has to take those photos. It's a type of portrait photography, but once you add a rock star and the energy of a fan, *that* is music photography.

Artists also need promotional photos, and often those are taken backstage before a show. For these, the band or artist may only have five minutes, but the photographer has to make a useable and artistic image in that short amount of time.

Lastly, is the show itself, and that is my "happy place."

At its best, music photography can remind someone how great a show was or make someone else wish they were there. It can even make you feel like you are there again, reliving that moment.

Music photography sounds so glamorous, but let's bring it back down to earth. I get asked all the time, and I mean *all the time*: "How do I get into photographing concerts?" I will answer that in a minute, but let's start with setting some realistic expectations.

People think they will meet their favorite rock stars and get to know their idols, which is so rare that I would say it's not true for most people. When you are photographing a show, you are working. It's a job. I have had to photograph meet & greets for artists I love, and I have wanted to ask if I could get a photo too, but that is not why I'm there. It's not why you're there either. These moments are not the time to be a fan; they are the time to be a professional photographer.

Photographing a live performance is the same thing—it has a few downsides of its own. Yes, you can enjoy the music, but often the music fades to the background and just becomes a rhythm you hear (through earplugs) that helps you time your shot. You're busy trying to document the show, and in most cases, you'd better move fast because you only get three songs to do it. You'll usually shoot from the photo pit in front of the stage, but sometimes you don't even get that! You may be shooting from the soundboard halfway back in the arena, or you may only get one song.

Music photography can be one of the hardest types of photography to do well because we don't control the show, the staging, the lighting, or the subject. One of the more controversial areas of photography is the pay system. Unless you are a successful tour photographer, there is just not much money in it, and often you are restricted on how you can use or monetize your photos because of a photo release the band's management will require you to sign before shooting. Still, with all of those ups and downs, when you do get that magic shot it's one of the most amazing feelings you will ever experience.

I did say I would tell you a bit more about getting into music photography, so here we go!

Only try to move into this field if you love music, and I mean *love* it. If you are looking to be famous or meet famous rock stars, then try weddings, headshots, or portraits instead. Getting into photographing music isn't easy, and they are not going to let you bring a professional camera into a big show simply because you want to build a portfolio.

Getting access requires you to be photographing on assignment for a media outlet like a magazine, blog, radio station, newspaper, or TV station. If you don't have that already lined up, then you will need to build up your portfolio and experience in small venues, nightclubs, and bars—places where you will be able to get in with a camera. Learn the skills required to photograph in extreme low light, with no flash, at high ISO settings, all while trying to keep the artist sharp and avoiding the clutter on the stage from ruining the photo. It's never a good look to have a mic stand coming out of someone's head.

Low-light action photography is challenging, but it is very rewarding, so cut your chops in the small venues. Practice as often as you can, and be ready for when you get your first chance to photograph a big tour. Those big shows will limit you to the standard "first three songs from the pit, no flash," so learn this genre with those restrictions in mind. That way you'll be prepared for the big leagues when the opportunity arises.

A bit of a warning before I finish, music photography is addicting, *very addicting*. So don't be surprised if, after your first show, you end up hooked. Once you've tried music photography, there is no other option.

SEAN BAGSHAW

I guess I would have to call myself a specialist. But specializing in photography has resulted from my main specialty: following my interests.

When I was beginning, I photographed to document climbing and mountaineering adventures because those were my main interests at the time. Then, photography itself became a central interest. I wanted to learn how to take better photos so I studied, experimented with, and practiced many types of photography.

As my skills developed, I found that exploring and photographing landscapes is what motivated me the most, so I narrowed my focus to just landscape photography and put all my energy into getting better at that.

As I spent time photographing the land, certain qualities of light, weather, and composition called to me more than others, so I became more deliberate about searching those out. In the early days of digital imaging, I was excited to suddenly have much more creative control over developing my images and immediately became immersed in learning digital developing skills.

I have always enjoyed both learning and sharing knowledge, which brought me to my first career as a middle school teacher.

When my comfort and knowledge with landscape photography and image developing reached a certain level, I followed my teaching inclination with photography as well.

Not to say that I am not influenced by the images I see, input of others, trends, or logical business choices and goals, but I'm mindful of how much weight I give to what others think and what the current trends are, preferring to focus mostly on what actually appeals to me photographically. I also prioritize business choices around what I will be most motivated to put my full effort into rather than what might be simply a soul-crushing way to make a buck.

So, without intending it, I became quite specialized in the type of photography I do, the vision and style of my images, and the model that guides my business. But I didn't necessarily choose those specialties or formally define them as part of any master plan. Rather, they have grown organically as a result of my main specialty—listening to, and following, the things that have been most interesting and motivating at any given point along the way.

MICHAEL PACHIS

My journey specializing in zoo photography was a combination of accident, necessity, and passion. With a looming retirement after forty years in the information technology business, my wife, Teri, smartly said, "You need to find something to do and it should be something creative."

I did not regard myself as a creative at all. I cannot draw, can't carry a tune in a bucket, and the only writing I did was technical memos.

However, this suggestion intrigued me. Could I be creative after a life-time of left-brain pursuits?

After a visit from my brother, who had a digital camera, I decided photography could be that creative outlet and it also has a tech aspect.

For Christmas 2010 I purchased my first DSLR, a Canon Rebel. Now the question was, "What do I shoot?"

Memphis has a world-class zoo twenty minutes from my house, I was an animal lover, and family medical issues were keeping me from traveling to wildlife locations.

At first, it was just a place to get familiar with the camera and have a nice outing. After a while, I began to wonder if it was possible to make high-impact photos of animals in a captive setting. My goal was to create images of animals that humans could connect with on an emotional level. As I started to get more serious about my images, I consumed online classes, podcasts, and joined the local camera club. Club competitions and critiques helped me home in on what makes a powerful image.

If you want to specialize in zoo photography, my first bit of advice is you must go often. It cannot be the occasional outing. You can get lucky from time to time, but I subscribe to the Sammonism: The harder I work, the luckier I get.

Frequent trips allow you to observe the physical layouts of the exhibits, the best sight lines and backgrounds to eliminate unnatural elements, the light at different times of the day, and when animals are most active. All are very important elements in capturing a special moment.

As for camera gear, I'd recommend a zoom lens in the 100–400mm range. When I shoot, I carry a second body with a 24–200mm zoom lens for wildlife exhibits where animals are closer to the public.

I'd also recommend a camera with good auto focus performance and sustained frame rates of six frames per second or more. Moments are fleeting, and the frame-to-frame position of the animal, or its interaction with another animal or its environment, can make the difference between a so-so shot and a stunning image.

At the Memphis Zoo, I shoot aperture priority to blur out barriers in front of the animals, as well as the backgrounds. I must pay attention to my shutter speed so that it stays high enough to avoid motion blur. I do this by constantly adjusting my ISO setting. And by the way, don't be afraid to turn that ISO up! Depending on your camera, experiment with the upper limit of the ISO that gets an acceptable image. With my Canon 5D Mark IV, I don't mind going up to 8,000 ISO. If you are comfortable with the exposure triangle, manual mode is also an option for setting the camera.

As I write about my specialty, my last bit of advice may seem strange…shoot other genres of photography. Even though my greatest body of work is zoo animals, I shoot macro, still life, street photography, abstract, and others. I think it keeps the creative juices flowing, in general, and you will be surprised by the ideas and techniques from other genres that can apply to your specialty. I have applied many ideas from human portraiture to my animal shots (hint, it's all about the eyes).

As Rick's mother said, "You never know who's watching." The Memphis Zoo became aware of my images through Instagram and local exhibitions of my works. Now I'm a volunteer photographer for the Memphis Zoo with behind-the-scenes access to the animals. My passion for creating images of animals is now helping further the zoo's mission of conservation and education.

The journey continues.

I want to thank my dear, late wife, Teri, for recognizing the creativity in me that I did not see in myself. Teri started me on this journey; she was my partner and muse. Even though she is not with us anymore, her love of the natural world still inspires me every day to capture the most engaging images I can create of our fellow creatures with whom we share this planet.

JUAN PONS

I've always been fascinated by the natural world, specifically wildlife.

For as long as I can remember, I've always wanted to study the natural world, get immersed in it and learn its secrets.

Photography for me in a way is a means to an end, and that end is to learn about the natural world. Photography gives me the excuse to spend untold hours immersed in the natural world– observing, learning, and ultimately capturing its essence. Without photography I am afraid I would not have the patience that nature requires to get intimate with it.

Photographing wildlife rejuvenates me like nothing else. The excitement and anticipation of trying to predict what a wild animal is about to do in order to capture it is what I find most captivating. But this all starts way before I press the shutter release button. Before I can hope to capture a worthwhile image of an animal, I do lots of research on my subject, I learn about its behavior, its preferred environments, its life and yearly cycles, its preferred foods, etc. I then use this information to locate them and make images that I feel tell the viewer something about my subjects.

I am motivated by new and meaningful experiences. It's that simple. Experiencing a new location, watching a new (to me) wildlife species, capturing a stunning sunrise, this is what drives me to go out and make images.

This is why nature and wildlife photography is so exciting: every time you go out it's a whole new experience.

DON KOMARECHKA

Photography has always been a tool that allows me to explore the world that I cannot see with my own eyes. This applies to infrared, astrophotography, and many other areas of exploration, including my favorite: close-up/macro photography. I had a childhood fascination with understanding not just how things worked, but why they worked, and looking at the "building blocks" of our natural world with a macro lens rekindled that childhood curiosity early on in my career.

That curiosity has evolved into some fairly specific niches where there is always more to explore, from the humble snowflake through to the bizarrely beautiful fluorescence of flowers. The photography is secondary to the satisfaction of curiosity, but only just barely.

I've also found that certain areas of photography that could be described as the "path less traveled" are inherently more unique, and it's easier for my work to stand out. I'm certainly capable of taking a good landscape photograph, but to what end? I feel little satisfaction knowing that I've taken a photo nearly identical to thousands of others. With macro photography, you can present a room full of photographers with the same flower and you'll get vastly different results.

Equipment is part of specializing, especially when reaching the extremes. Much more important, however, is discovering subjects worthy of your attention, sometimes even creating them yourself as an artist with two mutually exclusive skill sets.

Water droplet refraction photography is a perfect example; first you need to be a droplet sculptor; second, you need to be a photographer.

Most of the time spent in my studio with water droplets has nothing to do with my camera, but rather the creation of something worthy of my photographic attention.

The same is true for freezing soap bubbles, where the subject doesn't exist until you create it. Countless hours have been spent researching which flowers will fluoresce under UV lights, all to gather knowledge that makes the photographic process possible.

Effectively, there is no shortcut to a deep understanding of your subject. Casually picking up your camera and expecting great results in any photographic niche is impossible without this understanding, regardless of how eruditely you operate your equipment. Making mistakes is a definitive part of this process as well. You cannot gain the knowledge required solely in theory; you've got to have an abundance of head-scratching moments and ample time to seek answers through practical experimentation. The number of failed attempts at a subject far outweighs the successes, though we really shouldn't call them failures.

Let's call them steppingstones toward that future success.

I'm often referred to as "the snowflake guy." As I write these words, I have just come back inside from...photographing snowflakes. It's a niche I have become well known for, even having my images engraved into Canadian currency.

Having notoriety in an area of photography has advantages, where anyone around the globe needing your specialized skills will seek you out. I have shot stills and video for many documentary film projects, and this work continues. However, I don't shoot "just" snowflakes or even macro photography in general. Some of my best experiences with a camera in hand involve wildlife, auroras, and the night sky. No matter how good I am in areas outside of macro photography, I doubt I'll ever be known for anything else.

Being a big fish in a small pond, sometimes the *only* fish in that pond has clear advantages. How many photographers have images of flowers being electrocuted with 30,000 volts? If any of the billions of people on the planet have any interest in such an image, there are only a few places where they'll be able to find it.

If you can be better than your competition, you'll stand out immediately. The audience and demand for such an image is tiny, however, so you need to market yourself in your area of expertise extensively to ensure that the right people find your work.

Many people come to the world of macro photography because of their curiosity and love of nature. Some people come from a love of science, looking for a greater understanding of the world around them. Whatever the reason for your interest, embrace it. Use that passion to fuel your exploration, and to guide you into very specific areas of focus. Because of the amount of tinkering and problem solving you'll be doing to overcome both technical and creative problems, I can guarantee you a high level of frustration.

If you're not passionate enough about why you're exploring macro photography, it can be difficult to revel in your mistakes as part of the learning process. If, however, you love being immersed in your subject even without a camera, you'll enjoy the process contentedly enough to be happy with every challenge you face.

Remember, close-up photography covers some of the most diverse photographic subjects, from grains of sand and pollen to flowers, butterflies, and many other small natural objects.

Not every subject has a story to tell, but you can push beyond the simple "fascination factor" of your subject by trying to build a narrative into your image.

Shoot a flower from underneath, growing up toward the sun. Shoot grains of sand with a few natural rough diamonds, easily purchased on eBay for $20. Shoot a time-lapse of a flower blooming. Follow an ant around until you discover its mission for the day, and then find a way to build an image around it.

The universe at our feet is alive, and often easier to anthropomorphize than you think. Doing so will help people stay connected to your work. As otherworldly as it may become, it is always helpful to find some level of personal connection to it.

Finally, show people just how different this world is: take some behind-the-scenes images of your setups. This might include adding something for scale in a secondary image, to show your audience that these beautiful subjects are all around us, right under our noses, but are too small to appreciate with our own eyes.

Thank you again my friends for your insight and inspiration. You guys rock!

Speaking of saying, "Thank you," there's a book I recommend to photographers who are on a quest to become better businesspeople. It's a book that will also help them, as well as you and me, and just about everyone in life.

The book is *The Thank You Economy* by Gary Vaynerchuk. Check it out. After reading it, I guess that you will say "Thank you" more often.

YOUR MISSION

Carefully consider the pros and cons of specializing and not specializing. Do what works for you by following your heart.

11.

CREATING A
SENSE OF MYSTERY

When you destroy the mystery of the photograph,
you destroy the photograph.
— UNKNOWN

T he quote that opens this chapter is one of my favorite photog-
raphy-related adages. It's a concept that can be applied to
painting and music, as well.

When it comes to creating an artist image, it rings true, in most cases.
Of course, like everything else in life, it's not true all of the time.

Creating a sense of mystery in our photographs and art is a good
exercise. Let's examine a few techniques for reaching that goal when
taking a photograph, which can be applied to making a painting as well.

HIDE THE FACE

There are several methods for hiding a subject's face in a photograph.
You can tilt a hat down so that it covers the face or photograph a person
from behind.

Speaking of photographing a person from behind, imagine this: In
your hands, you are holding a color photograph of a blond-haired
woman who is standing in the center of what looks like a small living

room, illuminated by light streaking through the bare windows. She is wearing a formal, backless dress that touches the floor.

Paint is peeling off the walls and the metal radiators are covered with rust. The blades of a dusty ceiling fan hang limply, like a bloodhound's ears.

The stained carpet is frayed. This mystery woman looks as though she is about to take a step toward an open door.

Looking at this photograph, you may wonder: Why is this seemingly beautiful woman in the room and why is she wearing a formal dress? Perhaps most importantly, because she looks striking from behind, the viewer wonders what this woman may look like.

So this photograph (which you can see in my "What's Possible?" gallery on ricksammon.com) not only has a sense of mystery, but it also asks for the viewer's participation, and having the viewer's participation is one-way artists draw attention to their artwork.

WORK WITH SHADOWS

Here are some thoughts on the importance and effectiveness of shadows in a photograph. Shadows are the soul of the photograph. Shadows add a sense of depth and dimension to a picture, and a sense of mystery. Light illuminates and shadows define; without shadows, a picture falls flat. When it comes to fine art photography (which experts would actually call simply fine art), shadows are king. Think of your favorite landscape photographs. My guess is that they were taken early in the morning, or late in the day when the sun was low in the sky and casting captivating shadows.

Think of a favorite portrait or painting of a person, maybe Vermeer's *The Girl with a Pearl Earring*. It's the shadows on the girl's face that gives the painting an almost 3-D look—and those shadows create a sense of drama in the work of art.

When watching the scenes with Marlon Brando in his dark office in *The Godfather*, you can't see into his eyes. Why? Director Francis Ford Coppola used top lighting to cast shadows over the eyes, therefore creating a sense of mystery in the scenes.

ONLY SHOW HANDS, FEET, OR FACE

Showing only part of a person's body in a photograph creates a sense of mystery because the viewer tries to "fill in the blanks."

One example of this is in some advertisements for lipstick. You can see the woman's mouth and nose, but not the eyes—the most important part of a portrait. Basically, the subject is wearing a mask, so to speak, and masks prompt the question: What's behind the mask?

A photograph, taken while lying on one's back, that shows crossed, bare legs and feet also creates a sense of mystery, especially if the legs are those of woman and the toenails are painted bright red.

A close-up of a hand or hands, especially those of a baby or very old person, also prompts the viewer to think, perhaps about age.

SHOOT FOR A SILHOUETTE

A silhouette is the ultimate shadow shot because details are lost in the darkness. Still, we can see the person's profile if they are looking directly off to camera left or right. Here, too, our eyes search for more information about the subject.

TAKE AN INSTAGRAM-TYPE SHOT

Wide-angle pictures in which the person is tiny are popular on Instagram, where we can actually find works of art, as well as tons of cliché sunset and sunrise photos.

No matter how small a person is pictured in a scene, that person adds a sense of scale to the photograph. That tiny person can also create a sense of mystery and wonderment by asking the question: How did the person get there and what are they doing there?

ADD A SOFT-FOCUS VIGNETTE

My photographer friends Anne Belmont and Julie Lee sometimes add a soft-focus vignette to a flower image to create a more artistic and interesting effect—and it works beautifully. The vignette can be created in Photoshop or with an accessory called the Lens Baby, which attaches to a digital SLR or mirrorless camera like a lens.

GET UP CLOSE

Rust. I love it, and so do my photographer friends. I'm talking about close-shots of rust, which can produce wonderful, intriguing, and thought-provoking abstracts.

Why do we like abstracts? I found one answer on art-is-fun.com: abstract art gives you the freedom to explore the artwork and assign your own meaning to the piece. Abstract art can also make people uneasy because they don't automatically know what the art is "about" with just a cursory glance. Or they assume that because it doesn't look like anything, then it is not "about" anything.

ADD AN OBJECT

Imagine you are in the dilapidated room mentioned in the "Hide the face" section. In the room, you see an early 19th century upright piano, dusty keys cracked like dried mud, the varnish buckling in spots like blisters.

Now imagine the room without the piano. The piano—an object—adds a sense of mystery and interest to the scene. We wonder about not only the piano but about the piano player.

So adding/including an object can add a sense of mystery and interest to a photograph. The more interesting the object, the more interesting the photograph.

BLUR THE SCENE

When I give a presentation, I often ask the audience, "How many people have taken an out-of-focus picture?" Many people raise their hands. Then I ask, "How many people have deleted their out-of-focus pictures?" That question generates an almost unanimous laugh.

I go on: "Don't delete your out-of-focus pictures. One out-of-focus picture is a mistake; twenty out-of-focus pictures is a style.

Of course, I am joking with the audience, but there is some truth to what I say. Blurry and out-of-focus pictures can be a style. For example, in the early 1990s, a woman came to me with a portfolio of pictures taken at slow shutter speeds while riding a horse through a forest. The pictures showed trees blurred vertically…and beautifully and artfully. Had the pictures been taken at a slower or faster shutter speed, the pictures may not have been as effective in creating the feeling of motion.

I loved the images and encouraged the woman to do a book. She took my advice and had the book published. I'm sorry I forget her name. (If it's you and you are reading this book, please shoot me an email.)

I'd like to end this chapter with two more quotes that relate to the topic of the chapter:

A photograph is a secret about a secret.
The more it tells you the less you know.
— DIANE ARBUS

The mystery isn't in the technique, it's in each of us.
— HARRY CALLAHAN

YOUR MISSION
Set a goal to make five photographs that have a sense of mystery.

12.

PHOTOGRAPHY AND THE DEATH OF REALITY

"We all know that art is not truth.
Art is a lie that makes us realize the truth."
—PABLO PICASSO

In some of my seminars, I talk about "Photography and the Death of Reality," sharing photographs that look more like paintings than photographs, or photographs that have been enhanced in Photoshop or Lightroom and with plug-ins. You can see some of these images in my "What's Possible?" gallery on ricksammon.com.

Here's the gist of the concept. As in many other cases in this book, think about how these concepts relate to painting and other art forms.

"Photography and the Death of Reality" is not a new topic, but as we move more and more into digital darkroom enhancements, the topic becomes more and more important.

Before I go on, I'd like to share a story with you about Ansel Adams, relayed to me by one of his assistants, the talented John Sexton. He told me that a man wrote Ansel Adams a letter (condensed here): Dear Mr. Adams, I have your wonderful books. Your beautiful pictures of Yosemite inspired me to visit this National Park. However, when I got there, I was disappointed. The park does not look like that.

So much for reality.

Since the early days of photography, people with cameras have made images that don't represent reality, even when they tried. That's due, in part, to the way cameras record light, and how lenses bend light and compress or widen a scene or subject, not to mention that we see in 3-D and cameras see in 2-D and that our eyes have a dynamic range that is wider than a single digital file.

I am sharing this "Death of Reality" philosophy with you for three main reasons:

1) To encourage you to make your most creative images ever, and not to be afraid to follow your heart when it comes to making digital enhancements.

2) It's important to consider the reality of your photographs and the photographs of others, again asking yourself if you are a photographer or an artist.

3) I think it's important to realize that photographers are somewhat like magicians, or illusionists if you will. The creative process of image making is like the art of doing a magic trick. If you don't know the trick, the trick is amazing. If you do know the trick, you know that it's a relatively simple procedure.

When creating an image, consider Edgar Degas's philosophy: "A picture is a thing which requires as much knavery, as much malice, and as much vice as the perpetration of a crime."

I end my talk, "Photography and the Death of Reality," by saying that I could have called it *"Photography and the Birth of Creativity,"* because we live in such an exciting image-enhancing time.

YOUR MISSION
Don't be afraid to create your own reality with your photographs.

13.
WHERE TO GO FOR GREAT PHOTOGRAPHS & INSPIRATION

"Men go abroad to wonder at the heights of mountains, at the huge waves of the sea, at the long courses of rivers, at the vast compass of the ocean, at the circular motion of the stars, and they pass by themselves without wondering."
— SAINT AUGUSTINE

Antarctica. Africa. Alaska. Southeast Asia. The Galapagos. These destinations, for sure, are great places to go for great photographs and for inspiration for paintings, as well as for musical creations. On this latter note, the Beatles travelled to India for musical inspiration.

However, even if you travel to these far-away places, you may not get, for a variety of reasons, great photographs or artistic ideas. The weather could suck, the wildlife may not be active or may be out of sight, you might get sick, or you (especially if you are a beginner) may not have the photographic, technical, or artistic expertise to get compelling images.

As an example, I have some super-sharp photographs taken in Alaska of bald eagles flying at high speeds. They are tack sharp. I took these photographs on my fourth trip to Alaska. On my first few trips, many of my bald eagle images were soft or even out of focus.

I also have some amazing underwater photographs taken on 36-exposure rolls of film. The truth is that I only got one amazing shot per roll…if I was lucky.

Yes, distant lands can provide photographic—and personal—inspiration, but as Robert Pirsig said, "The only Zen you find on the tops of mountains is the Zen you bring up there."

In other words, you don't necessarily have to make a long trek to make artistic images on your creative image quest. Here are some suggestions for where to make artistic images closer to home. For each location I'll offer a mission/assignment.

As you will see, each of these locations is a good creative photo quest location. Although I offer photo tips, I am sure you will get the idea when it comes to painting, sketching, and so on.

LOCATION—BALLET STUDIO

IDEAS:
+ Work with mirrors and watch for reflections.
+ Capture the peak of action—a ballerina in mid-air.
+ Go for close-ups, maybe just a ballerina's shoes.
+ Try to capture gesture.
+ Offer your images in exchange for the shoot.

LOCATION—SUSHI RESTAURANT

IDEAS:
+ Adjust your aperture for shallow/deep depth-of-field.
+ Make the picture—arrange the sushi plate and sake cup.
+ Photograph the sushi chefs in action.
+ Offer your pictures in exchange for sushi. (I've done this!)

LOCATION—LOCAL FIREHOUSE

IDEAS:
- Start a photography project: Hometown Heroes.
- Take headshots and full-length shots of the firefighters wearing their gear.
- Ask if you can ride with the firefighters to document a fire.

LOCATION—JAZZ CLUB

IDEAS:
- Get permission to photograph first.
- Turn off your flash.
- Don't be afraid to boost your ISO—embrace the noise.
- Take wide-angle and close-up shots.
- Take detail shots of the instruments and the performers' hands.
- Move around (if possible) to vary your angle.
- Be aware of others; don't be annoying.
- Turn off your camera's LCD monitor.
- Don't forget to shoot some videos.

LOCATION—BOOK CLUB MEETING

IDEAS:
- Photograph the members by window light.
- Take close-ups of hands and books.

LOCATION—LOCAL BOTANICAL GARDEN

IDEAS:
- Get permission first, especially about tripod use.
- Pack a macro lens and maybe a ring light.
- Experiment with shallow/deep depth-of-field.
- Try natural light.
- Take wide-angle shots and try to tell the whole story.

LOCATION—NEARBY RIVER, POND, WATERFALL, OR STREAM

IDEAS:
- Become an expert on using an ND (neutral density filter).
- Try several different long exposures to see their effect on the moving water (you'll need a tripod, of course).
- Get down low and add a foreground element.

LOCATION—DRIVING RANGE

IDEAS:
- Set your camera on high frame rate to capture as much of a golfer's swing as possible.
- Shoot at a high frame rate to freeze the action.
- Talk to the golf pros to see if they need any photos of themselves or of the golf course.

LOCATION—CITY AT NIGHT

IDEAS:
- Use long shutter speeds to capture streaking taillights.
- Compose your pictures so red taillights are streaking away from you, as opposed to white headlights coming toward you.
- Wet down the pavement with a hose for cool reflections.
- Be careful. Remember what your mother told you: Wear white at night.

LOCATION—CHURCH, LIBRARY, TRAIN STATION, OR BUDDHIST TEMPLE

IDEAS:
- Get permission first.
- Use a wide-angle lens and embrace the distortion when you tilt up the lens. It's a cool effect.
- Photograph the light streaking through the windows. To create streaks of light in your photograph, rub your finger on your forehead, which will pick up a bit of oil. Streak your finger across a skylight filter on your lens. When you view your photograph, the streaks of light will look as if they are illuminated dust or smoke. It's a cool effect.
- Be sure to clean your filter for the next shot!
- Take pictures of candles and signs to help tell the story.

LOCATION—ANY STREET

IDEAS:

- Go for a walk after it rains. Photograph oil spots on the road, which can be very colorful.
- Boost the contrast and saturation of your oil spot shots for an even more colorful photograph.
- Don't underestimate the potential impact of your oil spot images. At one of my workshops, the workshop participants made some very colorful, original, and striking images of this subject.

I think watching movies is a wonderful way to get inspired—not only photographically (see my note about *Citizen Kane*, *The Fountainhead*, and *Sunset Boulevard* in **Chapter 5: The Rollercoaster Ride of Creatives**), but intellectually as well.

Watching moves about artists is especially inspiring. *Frida*, the story of Mexican artist Frida Kahlo, is one such example. This artist was amazing in her triumphs. I don't want to give anything away, so I will leave it at that.

The episode about Pablo Picasso in the *Genius* series by National Geographic is another source of artistic inspiration, although you probably don't want to end up like Picasso. Here, too, enough said.

You can find more movies about artists by doing a Google search: "films about artists."

I have one more suggestion. It's not a happy one, so you may want to skip the next few paragraphs. In fact, it might make you cry. However, it can be very rewarding.

There's an organization called, Now I Lay Me Down to Sleep (nowilaymedowntosleep.org). The group connects photographers like you with parents who have lost a child during birth.

I told you it was sad.

I am moved as I write this section, remembering a Photoshop request I accepted via email several years ago to make the lost child look more angelic, a request I accepted and one that brought some peace to the family.

And speaking of making someone grateful with a photograph, read what Cheryl Haggard, co-founder of Now I Lay Me Down to Sleep, said about the photograph of her lost son, Maddux: "*That night was the worst night of my life. But when I look at the images, I am not reminded of my worst night. I'm reminded of the beauty and blessings he brought.*"

Here's another place you can go for inspiration: your computer.

Of course, you can explore the creative options in Photoshop, Lightroom, and plug-ins, but here's another idea that might take you on a new path on your creative photo quest.

First, listen to a piece of music, perhaps *Moonlight Sonata*. Then go through your photo library and try to find an image—a peaceful and beautiful image—that expresses the mood and feeling of the piece.

Now listen to a hard-rock song or an intense jazz song and find an image that "speaks" to that music.

I got the idea of putting a photo with music during a live concert by Chick Corea, one of the best jazz keyboard players on the planet. During his performance, Chick had people come on stage and sit in a chair next to his piano. He then proceeded to play a musical "personality portrait" of the individual. He did this about six times. Each piece he played was different, and the audience, including me, felt that Chick captured the person's personality exquisitely.

At first, your mission may be challenging, but if you stick with it, I am sure you will find a photograph or photographs, or a painting or paintings, that fit the music.

Let's take that concept to the next level. Take a break from reading this book, go to YouTube, and type "collection of silent movies" in the Search bar.

Take a look—and listen—and then come back.

Welcome back!

In the early days of silent movies, live music was used to express the mood and feeling of the scene. Without the music, the film did not have the same "feel." One of the best examples I know that illustrates this idea is the 1927 film *Metropolis*, which I saw in the mid-1990s with a live orchestra at a local concert hall. The music was haunting in some scenes and added to the drama of the film.

So here's the idea, somewhat a reverse of the silent film music concept (movie first, music second): find a favorite piece of music and put together a slide show that fits the music. If the piece is *Moonlight Sonata*, find a collection of peaceful landscapes and seascape pictures or paintings. They don't need to be taken at night by moonlight; they only need to have a peaceful feeling.

Getting back to the "film-first" idea, if you have photographs or paintings from a trip, say photographs or paintings of bald eagles, whales, bears, waves, and snow-capped mountains from Alaska, find a piece of music that expresses joy and awe—perhaps a smooth jazz song or jazz standard, or a soft Santana song such as "Moonflower."

One note here: if you plan to publish your slide/music show on the web, be sure the music is not copyrighted. For royalty-free music, check out triplescoop.com.

In choosing music, keep in mind that music is a very personal choice—more so, I think, than with photography. The "wrong" kind of music can quickly turn off someone.

My parting words for this chapter: choose your music carefully.

Your Mission

Wherever you go, go with all your heart.
— Confucius

14.

KNOW YOUR AUDIENCE
AND BUILD YOUR BRAND

I don't care about the audience; I am the audience.
— LORD SNOWDON

I understand what Lord Snowdon is saying about his audience—that he really does not care what other people think of his work. That's a noble idea because we all need to follow our heart.

If you are a Lord and are independently wealthy, it's easy to not care about your audience. If you are like most photographers and artists, including myself, we definitely need to care about our audience, because it is the audience who chooses to follow a photographer or artist on social media, signs up for a workshop or seminar, buys a book or online class, and generally supports us.

This text in this chapter could have been included in **Chapter 2: What's Needed on the Photo Artist's Palette?** and in **Chapter 18: The Business of Being Creative**. I separated the topics of knowing your audience and building your brand because they are very important aspects of your photo quest.

KNOW YOUR AUDIENCE

My best advice for getting to know your audience is to listen and to treat everyone with respect.

Imagine you own and operate a small bakery in your town. Someone walks into your shop. If you: 1) listen to their request, 2) take the time to get to know them, 3) treat them with respect, and 4) have the goal of having them leave satisfied and with a smile, they'll come back—all because you put in the effort.

The same philosophy applies to posting stuff on social media and answering e-mails from strangers. In other words, be nice.

Once you get to know your audience, you want to build it so more people come into your equivalent of a small-town bakery. Here are some suggestions for doing just that:

1) Post regularly on social media sites, sharing educational, in-formative, and fun content. Don't underestimate "fun" content. Most people want to smile and laugh, so if you can bring a smile to someone's face, that's a good thing. When posting, add a link back to your "store" (your website). Also, ask a question. I have found that when I ask a question on Facebook, I get many more likes and much more interaction.

2) Post regularly on a blog and ask for feedback. In the post, add affiliate links (where you get a small commission) so you can make a few bucks for putting in the effort.

3) Give stuff—educational material—away for free. Your free stuff can be an e-book or an online class.

4) Be current. In your posts, stay topical. Follow trends in the pho-tography industry (or travel industry, if that is your field). Be-come an expert.

5) Tell stories. Rather than just sharing facts, weave them into a story. For example, in talking about getting to Antarctica, I could say: "It's a two-day journey over the Drake Passage, where the seas can have forty-foot swells." Or I could say: "On my two-day adventure from Ushuai, the southernmost city on the planet, to Antarctica, known as the white continent, we traveled over what some say are the roughest seas in the world. Here I learned about the two stages of seasickness. Stage One, you feel as though you are going to die. Stage Two, you wish you were dead!"

6) Think about your audience not only as customers but also as a family. I have done this on my workshops and photo tours, and I can tell you this works. Many repeat clients are more like family than customers, and some have even stayed at my house.

7) Start a podcast. Except for the small hosting fees, the only investment you need to make is that of your time. Here, too, knowing your audience is key.

8) Do free webinars. You can do these by yourself using webinar-hosting services, or you can do these with and for companies. For example, I have done webinars for NANPA (North American Nature Photography Association) that were beneficial for the organization and myself. I've also done webinars for plug-in companies with the same results. The benefit of working with a larger company than yours is that you'll have, of course, a larger audience.

9) Work with other pros. Have other pros write guest blog posts and share the spotlight on your podcast. Promote their work on social media sites. Make friends. As you promote other pros, they will, in turn, promote you.

In all of the above suggestions, keep in mind that your audience's attention span and time they have for reading your stuff is limited. Try to get to the point as soon as possible. That's easy for me today, while writing this book of more than 40,000 words.

One more thing about knowing your audience: when you are giving a live seminar or presentation, it's of the utmost importance to know your audience. You can't talk down to anyone in the room. And in fact, don't feel as though you are having a one-way conservation. Ask for feedback, even if it's at the end of your talk.

Here's something I learned in the ten-week Dale Carnegie course on public speaking: The most important thing in the first thirty seconds of a talk is... take a guess... think a bit... body language. Yes, move your arms and hands, use gestures. After you have the audience's attention, you can convey your message—with enthusiasm.

Don't Lose Your Audience

Want to lose part of your audience? Of course, you don't. There are three sure-fire ways to get people to stop following you, or worse still, to try to hurt your feelings and stir up a heated discussion: post stuff about guns, religion, and climate change.

Speaking of religion, one of my friends got a bad book review on Amazon because he thanked Jesus in the book.

I have found that even with solid facts, you can't change a person's mind who has the opposite opinion.

BUILD YOUR BRAND

Basically, your brand is you—to the public, not to your family and close friends. As Jeff Bezos, founder of Amazon, said, "Your brand is what other people say about you when you are not in the room."

Here's another way to look at your brand: It's your reputation.

Before "broadcasting" your brand, you need to build your brand. The key, I feel, is to be yourself, let your personality and passions shine through. Those attributes should be summed up in your mission statement or tag line.

My friend Art Wolfe's mission statement sums up what people will get from his books, workshops, and seminars: Explore Create Inspire.

In these three words, you get a good idea of why you want to hang out, in person or on the pages of one of his books, with Art.

When I worked in the advertising industry, we had meetings during which we discussed strategies, objectives, and tactics. In developing your brand, think about the ways in which you can spread the word (social media, for example), your objectives (filling workshops, selling books and prints, etc.), and your tactics (a daily practice for your business).

Another important step in building your brand is having a logo. If your brand takes off, you will not even need to use your name. The Nike Swoosh (a check mark shape) and the CBS eye are two good examples.

You can have a logo designed by an online logo designer. I had mine designed by Hudson Valley Graphic Design here in Croton-on-Hudson, New York. The process of creating a logo requires a lot of reflective thinking, which is a good thing!

Signatures can also become your logo. For a unique signature logo, check out fontbros.com. You can design a totally unique signature/logo there.

Well, my friend, if you know our audience and build your brand, you will be on your way to running a successful business, which will allow you to do what you love most: take pictures.

YOUR MISSION

Listen to your audience and speak to it with your mission statement.

15.

ANALYZE THIS

A photograph is usually looked at and seldom looked into.
— ANSEL ADAMS

Before reading this chapter, do a web search on Leonardo da Vinci's *The Last Supper* and Salvador Dalí's *The Sacrament of the Last Supper*. Take a good, long, hard look *into* these photographs. If you are at a desktop computer, maybe have them opened at the same time as you are reading this chapter.

After you have completed this chapter, go back to the photographs and, once again, look into them, and see if you notice anything new.

The idea here is to look into these paintings and see how the artists use creative techniques to draw the viewer into the scene, much like we, as photographers, need to use creative techniques to make compelling images. Those creative techniques include composition, exposure, lighting, gesture, depth, and most importantly, mood.

This chapter is more technical than the other chapters in this book. I included it because I think it will help you find your photographic and artistic voice. While reading about these techniques, consider how they apply to your photography and art.

Print a favorite photograph of yours, hold it in your hand, and look into it. Be aware of what you see. This analysis will help you determine the visual impact of your photograph and artwork. Don't rush this process. As I said in the **About This Book** section, slow down.

Let's first look into *The Last Supper*.

Before we get going, I need to thank my friend Ian Plant for sharing, in a wonderful presentation I attended, how the painting illustrates the idea of why one should break the rules of composition. The rule: dead center is deadly. Well, as Ian pointed out, Jesus's head—the most important element in the painting—is dead center in the frame. And no one has complained about Leonardo da Vinci's composition. Enough said.

Ian got me thinking, so I began to explore the painting. The following are some painting techniques (in addition to Ian's point about composition) that Leonardo used to create what some say is the most famous painting in the world.

Again, think about how you can apply these techniques to your photographs or a painting. If you can include all of these techniques in one image, you are indeed a master! But that is a challenging task.

For starters, try to use one or two of the following techniques when making a photograph or a painting. The result: the viewer will look into the image—and so will you.

SENSE OF DEPTH—The walls on the left and right of the painting produce a strong vanishing point that helps draw the viewer into the scene. The ceiling panels add to the effect.

A photographic example of a vanishing point is a photo of a railroad track photographed at a low angle with a wide-angle lens set at a small aperture (for maximum depth of field). The converging rails in the distance create the effect that the subject is "vanishing" into the distance.

The more depth you create in a photograph, the deeper someone will be drawn into it.

SYMMETRY—There are an even number of disciples to the left and right of Jesus, so the painting is balanced. Adding to the balance are the four panels on each wall.

In photography, balance works when it comes to reflections, such as a tree perfectly reflected in still water with the water line in the center of the frame (see the cover of my *Photo Therapy* book).

Another example of symmetry would be a photograph of a family of thirteen having a picnic at a long table with six family members sitting to the left and six to the right of the head of the family, all seated on the same side of the table, as in *The Last Supper* where everyone is sitting on the same side of the table. Da Vinci also used symmetry in the *Vitruvian Man*.

There are basically three types of symmetry/balance:

1) Symmetrical asymmetrical, where the subjects/elements are not the same, but they are equally balanced (as seen in *The Last Supper*);
2) Symmetrical balance, in which the subject is basically the same on the left and the right (*Vitruvian Man* and a tree reflected in a still pond); and
3) Radial balance, illustrated by a daisy, pinwheel, or the sun (which have points or rays being equal in length from the center).

So, composing for symmetry is a good composition technique.

SENSE OF MYSTERY—We wonder what the apostles are saying to each other after Jesus shared the news about his betrayal. That feeling creates a sense of mystery in the painting. We wonder, "Who is the betrayer?"

Adding a sense of mystery adds interest to a photograph. Even small elements in a painting or photograph can add to the sense of mystery. For example, looking very closely at the painting, we notice that there is a spilled saltshaker near Judas. In some cultures, that symbolizes bad luck. So we wonder if Leonardo da Vinci was illustrating to the viewer that bad things were to come.

When you are compositing a picture, carefully consider that each and every element can say or symbolize something, and how it might add a sense of mystery to your image.

Read **Chapter 11: Creating a Sense of Mystery** for some ideas on this topic.

SEPARATION—Separation is important in painting, as well as in photography. We need to separate subjects/items so they don't get lost in the background and among each other. Notice how Jesus's head is separated from the scene by the window behind him. Each apostle's head is also clearly separated in the painting. Most of the hands are also nicely separated from the surrounding areas.

Separation is needed in a two-dimensional (height and width) image to create a sense of depth, which we see in a three-dimensional (height, width, and depth) scene.

I'll add another observation and tip here. Notice that the horizon line behind Jesus is not going through his neck. That would have been a classic no-no because it basically "decapitates" the subject. So, don't decapitate the subject with the horizon line, especially when photographing at the beach.

GESTURE—Gesture (facial expressions, head, hand, and body position) is important in people photography. Gesture tells a story; here, among the apostles, it's one of questioning. But Jesus's gestures are different, conveying a sense of peace.

When you are photographing, look for gestures—not only in people, but also in the "gesture" of waves, branches, and fields of long grass, and of course, in animals.

LIGHTING—The lighting on the faces of the apostles is fairly even throughout the painting. There are no harsh shadows. Jesus's face is shaded a bit. What's more, the room is perfectly "exposed" as is the background.

To create a photograph like this, one would need several soft boxes to evenly light the subject and would need to use HDR (high dynamic range) photography to get a good exposure of the scenes inside the room and out.

In addition, a photographer would need to use a wide-angle lens set at a small aperture to get everything in focus. Or, focus stacking or creating a composite could be used to create great depth of field.

The idea here is to study the work of the master painters and to apply their techniques to your photography.

MOOD & FEELING—The most important element in a painting or photograph is the mood or feeling one gets from viewing it. The subtle tones and gestures of the subjects in *The Last Supper* convey the mood of the moment, as does the setting (dinner table in a small, intimate room).

When you are making a picture, remember the 3Ms philosophy: mood matters most.

BRIGHTNESS—When viewing a painting or photograph, our eyes are usually drawn to the brightest part of the scene. In the case of *The Last Supper*, it's the window behind Jesus. In looking at the window, we are immediately drawn to Jesus's face.

If you want the viewer of your photograph to be drawn to the most important subject in the frame, make it the brightest object in the frame.

That being said, the opposite is also true; our eyes can also be drawn to the darkest part of a scene. For example, if we take a photograph of a bison in the snow, our eyes are drawn to the bison.

Our eyes are also drawn to areas in a painting or photograph that have the most contrast. In *The Last Supper*, the strongest contrast is dead center, Jesus's darker head against the bright window.

TONES—Color wise, no single apostle stands out in the frame. That's because no one garment is more or less colorful than the next, in addition to the fact that they all have the same brightness value.

If you want that effect when taking a group or family portrait, coordinate the clothes in advance, and evenly light the entire group. If you are photographing a field of flowers and want that effect, compose the scene so no one flower, or group of flowers, stands out in the frame.

In *The Last Supper*, and in many photographs, even tones work perfectly. However, just like with brightness value, the opposite is true.

If you want one subject to stand out, make it more colorful in the scene. That can be accomplished by selectively using Saturation with the Adjustment Brush in Photoshop and Lightroom. If you are photographing a group of people, have the person you want to stand out wear a more colorful dress, shirt, or jacket.

On that note, here's an old photography adage: If you want a subject to stand out in the scene, have him or her wear red.

SUBJECT—Simply put, never underestimate the importance of a good/interesting subject. Needless to say, Jesus is an interesting subject.

When making a photograph, ask yourself if you think the subject is interesting. If it's not, ask how you can make it more interesting. For example, a portrait of a cheetah in Africa might be nice, but an action shot of a cheetah chasing an impala is more interesting.

When photographing a person, gesture can make a portrait more interesting. One example: When Karsh of Ottawa was photographing Winston Churchill, he wanted an interesting portrait; he wanted to capture the power and determination of the man. During the portrait session, Churchill was smoking a cigar. Right before Karsh snapped the photo, he quickly took away Churchill's cigar. Do a Google search to see Churchill's expression, captured exquisitely by Karsh.

Now it's time to look *into* Salvador Dalí's *The Sacrament of the Last Supper*. Again, take your time. Look into the painting.

You will see that the artist used the same techniques listed above to achieve the same effects, although the mood and feeling of the painting is totally different.

Many of the aforementioned techniques, combined or used by themselves, create one of the most important elements in painting and photography: a focal point (the area in the painting/photograph where our eye is immediately drawn).

Composition and depth of field also come into play when it comes to creating a focal point. One of the "rules" of composition is to imagine a tic-tac-toe grid over the frame and to compose the scene so the main subject, the focal point, is placed where lines intersect.

But heck, you did not write the "rules" of composition, so you don't need to follow them. They are, however, a good starting point.

When it comes to depth of field (how much of a scene is in focus in front of and behind a subject), the more out of focus the area around the main subject becomes, the more our eye is drawn to the focal point.

We can reduce the depth of field by using a telephoto lens, moving closer to a subject, and by selecting a wide aperture setting. The longer the lens and the wider the aperture, the less depth of field we have.

We can also reduce the depth of field in Photoshop by adding a blur around the main subject, creating what is called a bokeh effect.

Here's a good and creative technique for determining the focus point in a painting or photograph. Hold it or view it close to your face. Now close your eyes. Open your eyes very slowly. In most cases, your eyes will go to the focal point. Of course, you may be looking at a painting or photograph with no focal point, which does not mean it's a bad work of art. Jackson Pollock's later works of art—drips, drabs, and splatters of paint—had no focal point, and they worked!

Here's a question: What's the focal point of Vermeer's *Girl with a Pearl Earring* or Leonardo da Vinci's *Mona Lisa*?

Some may say that the subject is the focal point in each painting. Others may say it's the captivating eyes because the eyes are usually the first things we notice in a painting or photograph.

Before I go on: the next time you are in the supermarket checkout line, look into the photographs of the models on the covers of the fashion and beauty magazines. Notice the brightness of their eyes. In many cases, the art directors of the magazines have retouched the eyes to make them the brightest part of the image area, so your eyes are drawn to their eyes...to make a connection.

Okay, back to the paintings. In the case of the *Mona Lisa*, we are also drawn to the mouth. At times, it seems as though the subject is smiling, and at other times it appears that she is not. This has been called, "the catchable smile."

The smile or no-smile effect has to do with the viewing distance and the point in the painting at which you are looking.

More about this ingenious effect, and more about how and what we see in a painting or photograph, can be found in Margaret Livingstone's wonderful book *Vision and Art: The Biology of Seeing*.

YOUR MISSION
Look into, not at, your art.

16.
WITH A LITTLE HELP FROM MY FRIENDS

A real friend is one who walks in
when the rest of the world walks out.
— WALTER WINCHELL

I'm a "wealthy" guy. I have a wealth of friends who enrich my life in professional and personal ways. So, I am a lucky guy, too.

In this chapter, some of those friends offer advice that I feel will help you find your photographic and artistic voice, and you can take that to the bank. Read on and deposit their words of wisdom in your creative soul.

TONY L. CORBELL

In thinking back on my forty years in photography, I am reminded of a conversation I had one afternoon several years ago that produced an unexpected result and realization for me.

I was having lunch with my sister and one of her good friends asked, "Is your brother a famous photographer?" My sister's response was interesting. She said, "No I don't think so, but he is good friends with most of the famous photographers out there."

That afternoon, it struck me: while I don't feel as though I have any true "greatness" in me, I have done a decent job of surrounding myself with "greatness," and it has mattered more than I ever knew.

In my personal quest for finding my photographic voice, I have come to realize that my voice did not come entirely from within. Rather, it was the result of years and years of paying attention to, and learning from, those photographers that I admired and respected, regardless of their genre of work.

Comments and critiques from National Geographic documentary photographers, sports shooters, landscape photographers, fashion photographers, editorial photographers and food photographers all had a hand in my development as a photographer.

My voice, or in my case, my lack of a defined voice, came largely from these pros and their input in my life. I never felt that I fit into a niche or genre. I always felt I am just a photographer who understands light pretty well and will take on just about any photographic job or project if it is interesting.

At a commencement speech for one of the major photographic schools several years ago, I delivered a message on the importance of making connections. The students from that school, and for that matter all kinds of schools, make life-long connections and friendships, and these kinds of relationships made in these conditions will almost always stand the test of time. They will photograph each other's weddings, family portraits and children. They will assist each other on commercial shoots, and generally be sounding boards for each other throughout much of their professional careers.

I don't know of any working professional photographer who doesn't have colleagues or friends that they can't call on anywhere, at any time, for advice, tips, techniques, or any other kinds of help that might be needed.

"Connections!" That is the name of the game and it can be vital to ensure your success.

I don't know when it was that I started recognizing the importance of my photographic connections, but about the time my career started doing well is about the time that I made the observation. It was then I knew the importance of these connections.

As a result, I would always try to be as good at helping others as they were at helping me. But please understand that it is not about keeping score. You help from the heart and it will come back to you.

I remember a great photographer and friend from Oregon saying that we cannot "work in a vacuum, all alone, or our work will simply suck." That's pretty funny, but it's also pretty true.

I would advise photographers to, of course, follow their passion, find personal projects that speak to the heart and work, work, work, to make the images from these projects the very best they possibly can.

The great documentary photographer Dorothea Lange said, "Pick a theme and work it to exhaustion...the subject must be something you truly love or truly hate." That is the best way to find your passion and your voice. It will aid in your lifelong quest, not only your photo quest.

I will close with my own little expression: "You can take an average picture of an extraordinary thing, or an extraordinary picture of an average thing. It is entirely up to you and your vision."

ANNE BELMONT

I come to the photography world with a unique perspective. My first career was as an art therapist, and that career has had a major influence on how I approach and teach photography today.

What is art therapy? Art therapy strives to help the individual explore their emotions, develop self-awareness, and help resolve emotional conflict through the process of creating art.

A licensed art therapist helps others to understand the unconscious meaning behind their art and recognizes that the creative process itself is therapeutic and healing. A variety of mediums can be used, among them drawing, painting, collage, clay, and of course photography.

During my study and practice of art therapy, I delved deeply into understanding the creative process. Working predominantly with children, I became fascinated with how creativity was so alive and well in the lives of children but then often disappeared in the lives of adults.

As my photography career and my teaching evolved, I became interested in helping adults rediscover that creativity. I began to realize I had the valuable tools to help others connect more emotionally with their work, take joy in the process of creating, find their authentic voice as an artist, and rediscover creativity in the process.

An essential component in the creative process is slowing down and becoming more mindful in our approach to photography. We need dedicated time to create and to be creative. Relax, take a deep breath, and immerse yourself in the process. Rather than rushing from one subject to the next collecting images, spend time looking for a subject that speaks to you.

Ask yourself: What is drawing me to this subject? What story do I see? What emotions do I feel? Your way of seeing a subject is uniquely yours and comes from your personal history—your way of seeing the world, your emotional road map, the joys and losses, and all you have experienced in life. Just as your story is unique to you, the viewer of your image may see a totally different story based on their personal history. This is the beauty of art.

Spend time with your subject, exploring and photographing it in many different ways to make that story come to life. This is where the creativity emerges, and the "Aha!" moments happen. Don't be afraid to make mistakes—those mistakes are how we grow and learn and are an essential part of the creative process.

Creativity will begin to flow when we take this time and begin to get into that important dance with our subject.

If you watch a young child immersed in painting at an easel, you will realize that it is the process of painting and creating that is all-important to the child. Once the child leaves the easel, they forget about the painting.

As adults, we need to recapture some of that pure joy of creating and experimenting freely, the joy of being in the moment. I often tell my students to play like a three-year-old—play, experiment, and try new things. If we begin to see the world with the same sense of awe and wonder as a young child—as if we are seeing it for the first time—we will bring joy back into the process.

When I started practicing this in my own work, I started connecting with my subjects more intimately. As I look through my viewfinder, the beauty of my subject can totally captivate me. I am in a world all my own and unaware of what is happening around me. I am in that dance. It might be the luscious color, the gentle curves of the petals of a flower, the way the light is falling on my subject that draws me into that dance. An hour can pass without notice and I am still photographing the same flower, drawing deeper and deeper into my subject, and making new discoveries along the way. Had I noticed that beautiful curve of the stem before? Did I see the patterning underneath the flower? Did I see the beautiful gesture of the petal as if it were beckoning me when I move around to the side?

By staying present and staying with my subject, I develop a

relationship with it, and everything flows from there—the stories, the ideas, and the emotion. This takes time and this is precisely why we need time and practice. This magic will not happen by taking a quick image and walking away.

To me, the process of creating is more important than the finished image, it is what stays with me long after the image is done. The image serves to remind me of how much I enjoyed that time with my subject and my experience in nature.

So, as Rick suggests in his opening words in the **About This Book** section, slow down.

Play like that three-year-old! Bring back the joy!

ERIN BABNIK

"Exploration is the key to creativity. The more that you find to photograph, the more that you find yourself."

I first wrote these words for an article that was published a couple of years ago, but they represent a guiding philosophy that many creative photographers embrace: the notion that ideas come from experience.

The exact opposite belief would be that ideas come from some spark of genius that magically inhabits the brain of a lucky individual, and you either have the spark or you don't. On the contrary, creativity is earned, not bestowed, or inherited. The potential for having photographic ideas expands with each new experience behind the camera, especially if that experience is exploratory.

Venturing into unknown territory, experimenting with possibilities, and trying to solve problems without having any guarantees of success are all challenging but rewarding paths toward creative growth.

As layers of experiences accumulate, they tend to incubate in the mind, and sometimes an idea emerges out of that foundation like a bolt of lightning. In that case, the idea may seem like a eureka moment coming from nowhere, but usually it's possible to reflect upon all of the experiences that fed into that moment and to appreciate the connections that took time to develop.

Therefore, the best habits that a creative photographer can form are those that break other habits, that challenge the mind, and that open doors to new experiences.

KAREN HUTTON

A strong voice is inestimably powerful. Whether you're referring to a speaking voice (which I taught for twenty-five years to TV/radio news broadcasters), a photographic voice, an artist's voice, a writer's voice, or whatever, being able to make yourself seen and heard in the way your soul wants to not only makes you more effective, it's life-changing. It's life affirming. It sets a wave in motion that creates its own gravitational force; drawing to you the things, people, and experiences that make your spirit soar and life worth living.

I know, because I've seen it happen hundreds of times, and experienced it myself. I think it's magical.

When you're truly able to show up with a full, rich, and resonant voice in whatever you create, it becomes your signature: the signage of you.

In photography, I think of "signature" as an imprint of who you are, visibly embedded into the pixels of your images. Your artistic voice conveys your unique point of view, your special way of seeing the world and what's important in it, complete with subtle nuances, a palpable vibe, and all sung in a voice that can only be yours.

But how the heck do you get there?

Know Yourself

One of the most interesting things I learned over a long road of finding my own voice and teaching others to discover their own is that unleashing a powerful, resonant, authentic *speaking* voice takes pretty much all the same tools as unlocking your expressive one. It's actually a simple, practical process—and yeah, kind of a magical one, too.

But here's the deal: you have to get to know yourself and learn to *be* that. No matter what.

For starters, preparation is key. You can't call up something as mercurial as your muse (who *always* speaks with an authentic voice and has great ideas if you can just quiet your mind long enough to listen).

So you have to shift gears. Quiet your brain and become more mindful. Slow the breath, taking it way down low in the body, release all that distracting mind chatter, get yourself grounded and focused. You have to become more settled into your body, comfortably at ease in that lovely space inside where you can sense, look, listen, and feel what your muse has to say.

Some people use meditation techniques to get there, some use music. I have my own process, which I teach people in workshops and retreats. However you do it, this part of the prep is both physical and energetic. They work together. Personally, if I don't take this moment before I head out to shoot, or can't make the shift along the way, I can pretty much count on a "delete-athon" when I get home.

THE CREATIVE ARC

Creating in this way means working in what I call a "creative arc." It works from the inside out and is meant to run in a delicious, continuous flow. By the way, this is a completely natural process, not just something I made up.

It goes something like this:

1. Concept:
   + You have an idea, a desire, and a vision that you want to create. It starts the whole process.
2. Choose:
   + You decide where to go and set up the shoot, or whatever outer prep you need to do. Maybe that's just picking up your camera and walking outside; maybe it's setting up an entire production shoot.
3. Act:
   + You take the photo. (Inspiration must be acted upon for it to manifest!)

4. Verify

- You verify your results (in the moment or later on, depending upon the scope of the moment/project), meaning that you decide if the image floats your boat. Do you like it? Was it successful? Does it have the basic idea in there somewhere? Whether it's a sketch of an idea or the final, complete thought...did it work?

- Based upon *that* determination, where to next? *Important:* do not judge yourself harshly at this point! This is a delicate step, and one where the entire system can crash and burn. The goal is to keep an open mind and simply decide if something worked or not... and where to take it next. *not* to slap yourself around! Keep the flow going and keep listening to your muse.

5. Adjust, rinse, repeat

- Let a new idea about where to take your idea bubble up, and then act on and complete it. Rinse and repeat, always with your slowed breath, quiet mind, and finely tuned ears that always listen for the whispers of your muse. It's fun, it's playful, and it feels really good to work this way. It's how we did it as kids, expressing with our native genius.

- The creative process is fluid, it adjusts course constantly. The thing that keeps it flowing is an open mind; the thing that stops it cold is snarky personal judgment, which feels horrible. This stage requires that you roll with the former, an open mind that is in it to *play*! And be patient with yourself. Not kidding. Bags and bags of patience are required in the early stages.

WHAT DO YOU LOVE
AND WHY DOES IT MATTER?

As I said, finding your voice in anything, really, means learning about yourself. In good measure, it's about discovering what you love most, following that without blinking, and converting it into your work. And that, my friends, is what separates artists from copyists.

Art is an expression. It's emotional. It's encompassing. It's unique and original, simply by virtue of uncompromisingly bearing your mark. Creating it isn't always comfortable. Artists constantly push themselves to see more, and see differently. It's this constant quest to break patterns and let something more divine than us pour through us and into our work, which is why, over the ages, artists have always been amongst those to whom others look for inspiration. If your work doesn't make someone feel something when they see it, then what's the point?

To do that, you have to feel something. And it has to be specific, or it won't embed itself into your work.

How does it work? Well, by following what you love, by exploring the world around you through that lens, it reveals things you probably missed before. It'll teach you what catches your eye and captures your imagination, show you what you love to see, how you love to see it, how you feel about it, and pretty soon, you won't be able to help telling that story in your own spectacular voice.

It's a highly personal journey and it'll teach you an incredible amount about yourself—if you don't chicken out. It takes courage. Like I say, doing this will take you to new places, where status quo does not have a hall pass!

Once you find something you love, something that captures your attention, focus on it. Explore it, play with it, love on it. Be willing to experiment, making images that are more like sketches than finished products. Explore how to tell the story in a way that gives you chills. That's how you know you've discovered the heart of it.

Your quiet, focused mind, carefully listening to your muse, and your willingness to suspend your own snarky judgments along the way, will eventually result in a physical sensation—a rush of some sort—that will confirm you're there. In that magical, heightened state that is the ultimate "zone of creativity." And it's where your artistic voice lives.

Remember, the best art—and photography—is emotional. It takes knowing yourself well to create works like that, along with a very specific set of choices to make the vision clear.

GO. NOW. Search out what you love, what makes you feel amazing, and photograph through *that* lens!

It's a recipe that works as well for life as it does for photography!

DAVE DEBAEREMAEKER

Creativity, like everything else, is a journey, or as Rick puts it, a "photo quest."

It is a mindset to reject the world as it is and embrace the world in your head. It is a skill that can be nurtured and learned, and that gets stronger over time. It can, however, be rather difficult to know where to start on this journey. The answer is, of course, at the beginning.

During childhood, we are all naturally creative. During our play-times, we constantly create stories and imaginary environments where we can explore with reckless abandon, free from the restrictions of the real world—free of the responsibilities, free of the rules of the adults, and free of our limitations as kids. We can't fly in the real world, but in our imaginations, we could. All that imaginative play is just creativity at work.

As we grew up, many of us lost touch with that childlike creativity. As the saying goes: "When I was a child, I spoke as a child, but when I grew up, I put away childish things." There are many reasons for this: the socially awkward crucible that is high school, pressure to fit in with friends, seeking approval from a boss or a romantic interest. Over time, we can develop an aversion to standing out, to expressing ourselves with our imaginations and our creativity. Over time, it withers on the vine.

IGNORE THE OPINIONS OF OTHERS
We all want approval from our peers. It is natural. As we grow up, and social pressure grows, we tend to take risks to express ourselves, lest we stand out and not be accepted. This is especially true in the age of social media, where likes and followers rule. In that environment, it can be very stressful to put work out into the world that we are not sure will resonate with our peer groups.

The way around this is to ignore the opinions of others. You don't need to publish everything you create to the world. It is okay for your creativity to remain private while you are mastering new skills and techniques.

They say the only difference between amateurs and professionals is that professionals never share their mistakes. They still make them. They make many mistakes; you just may never see them. It is okay to keep your mistakes to yourself. Self-editing is an important skill, too.

Another roadblock for creativity is the fear of failure. Our time is limited, so it can be hard to justify working on something that has a high risk of failure. Creativity is risky. There's no guarantee that following an idea will lead to success. However, that misses the point.

The purpose of pursuing creativity is not the finished product. It is the journey in getting there. There is value in taking that journey whether you produce compelling work or not.

Learning To Feed Your Soul

This may come as a shock to the social media sensibilities many of us operate under, but creativity is not a popularity contest. I would argue that seeking popularity is the antithesis of creativity.

Creativity is an expression of your inner world in a unique way—your unique way. Only you can create your art. It is taking your unique experience, combining it with your unique view of the world, mixing it up, and applying it to your art. As such, it is singularly yours.

The problem is that we tend not to be in touch with our experiences. So much of our lives just glances off of us, and we rarely stop to contemplate what makes me "me," or what makes you "you." This sort of introspection can be uncomfortable, but it is a critical part of the creation process. Without introspection, it is hard to know how we speak with our creative voice, or if we merely puppet others' thoughts and opinions.

By figuring out what makes us individuals, we can start to embrace the things that impact us. That feeds our soul. Once we know what feeds us, what drives us, we can permit ourselves to pour those aspects into our art.

Once we do that, we can free ourselves to create the things we long to create.

STEVEN INGLIMA

Human beings have desired to communicate since the dawn of our existence. Perhaps simultaneously with the evolution of language came a desperate need to communicate with images. Of the five known senses, vision perceives and conveys our reality at the greatest distances from ourselves. Unaided, it gives us the power to see things many times further than we can taste, touch, smell, or hear. It provides us with our greatest security and encodes a large component of what we can consider our reality.

Drawings on the walls of caves have survived thousands of years and since before the invention of paper, depicting the life of their artists. They attest to our deep-seated need to connect with others about what we see and experience. These early drawings were created with a deliberate purpose. These are documents that show events and explain the life of some of our early ancestors. Every drawing involves a set of deliberate actions to make a deliberately crafted image.

Cave drawings evolved into more portable paper drawings, and then more detailed paintings. The human hand was the proto tool that allowed the creation of those images, until the advent of chemically based, light-sensitive imaging, or photography, which means (from the Greek) "light graph" or "light drawing." The word "photography" was created from the Greek roots φωτός (phōtos), genitive of φῶς (phōs), or "light," and γραφή (graphé) or "representation by means of lines" or "drawing," together meaning "drawing with light."

So, with the advent of our ability to create optically accurate and physically durable images with the use of a camera, humans had created and perfected an imaging technique that removed the subjective tool of our hands and replaced it with the more objective science of optics and light-sensitive surfaces. Now, a photograph could be captured without any specific idea, emotion, or communication objective, other than the creation of the image itself…even if by complete accident.

The possibility of this happening eventually increases the likelihood of it happening, and with it, the reduction of purposeful content within many images. More photographs have been captured this last year than in all of the years that the craft has been in existence. That is a staggering thought to contemplate. It also means that many of these images are simply documents to verify our presence at an event, like a selfie, or to remember some component within the frame for a later time. There is a gap between the utility of a document and the purposeful creation of an image whose existence has been crafted with a purpose to evoke emotion or communicate the love of the visual abstract in our natural world.

Photographs can convey a gradient hierarchy of importance, from virtually nothing to very significant.

LEVEL 1—PURPOSE

Almost every photograph, unless taken by accident, will have a purpose. It might be as utilitarian as recording the price of an item in the supermarket. It will have no other purpose, and thus is limited to this perhaps first level of importance. Its purpose is likely only being evident to the photographer who has captured that image.

LEVEL 2—PREMISE

The next level of importance will be a photograph with an evident premise. You should be able to establish the premise of the photograph within five seconds. Commercial photography, for instance, must have a premise. It must convince the viewer that the product has utility, practicality, and value. So this kind of photograph has both a purpose and a premise. We can think of a photograph's premise as its evident reason for being, and it is self-evident. Its premise is the clear reason why it was captured and created.

LEVEL 3—SIGNIFICANCE

Beyond the premise of the photograph is whether or not it has significance. A photograph that has significance can change the way we view an event, evoking deep emotion; or providing such a unique view of something as to change the way we see this scene, object, event, etc. At its most significant, a significant photograph might even change the course of history. Photographs can have significance for a variety of reasons:

1) An abstract photograph can have significance in the profound beauty of what it conveys, or a deeply personal vision of the artist that moves the viewer. Typically, in order to convey emotion in the photograph, it is likely that we as photographers will have to experience it in the capture and creation of that photograph. Then, should viewers experience a deep emotional response when viewing, there is now a significant connection made between the creator and the viewer.

2) Some photographs have significance for historical reasons—the building of bridges, skyscrapers, dams; or the plight of migrant workers; images of the Dust Bowl; scenes from the Great Depression, etc. Such images populate our national archives as documents to preserve historical events, states of being, conditions of our population, etc. We may catch key national figures in moments that change their fate, such as being caught in a lie or performing an act of great humanity.

3) Photographs have significance for social change reasons. When a single photograph can unify many people as to the horror of a war, the cruelty of a tyrant, or the slaughter or poor treatment of animals, etc., this can have the effect of mobilizing action. The significance of that image cannot be overstated. There are many that believe that two photographs taken in the Vietnam War were compelling enough to change our involvement in that conflict.

Like Rick, I like quotes. Here are a few of my favorites:

> To put it another way, the best photograph is that in which form and content are deeply interrelated where one discovers the meaning through the form and the form through the meaning....
> —CHARLES HARBUTT

> If you want to write you should learn the alphabet. You write and write and in the end you have a beautiful, perfect alphabet. But it isn't the alphabet that is important. The important thing is what you are writing, what you are expressing. The same thing goes for photography. Photographs can be technically perfect and even beautiful, but they have no expression.
> —ANDRE KERTESZ

> Technology doesn't really change photography, it just makes it available to more people, which means there's going to be much, much more really terrible pictures taken or pictures that are totally dependent on subject, which is all, all right.
> If you were at the scene when the Hindenburg caught on fire, and you took a picture of it, that's a great photograph. But that does not make you a great photographer, because you can't repeat that in everyday things. Great photographers consistently are able to make something in a style that's personal to themselves. My pictures don't depend on extreme sharpness. They depend on the composition and on the subject and on the way I see it.
> —KEN VAN SICKLE

> A photograph that is simply nothing more than a drive-by shooting probably has no premise.
> —STEVEN INGLIMA

Also, like Rick, I like to give photographers "missions." Here is mine for you: Your mission, should you choose to accept it, is to take the time to deliberate on *why* you feel inspired about what you see, and try to ensure that this is featured and evident in any image that you create. It's not an impossible mission.

IAN PLANT

Photography can make someone more aware. Successful photography requires the photographer to open his or her senses to the surrounding world. It requires an immersive approach, to seek a better understanding of the subject and attunement to its rhythms.

Photography can make someone more satisfied. There is a sense of completion when an artistic idea is given flight: starting as an abstract concept in the mind of the photographer, nurtured and tinkered with until all of the variables are worked out, then ultimately birthed into reality. There is nothing more satisfying than the act of creation, and the photographer engages in this act every time the shutter button is pressed.

Photography can make someone more whimsical. Photography is ultimately about discovery, and an exaltation of the magic of the moment. Chaos is the crucible of photography, and when random elements align to produce something worthy of capture, the photographer must seize the moment and pluck it from reality. The photographer must be playful and unpredictable in order to stay one step ahead of our capricious world.

GREG VAUGHN

A young woman on one of my workshops was there specifically for the therapeutic value of doing photography. Her mother had recently passed after long suffering from Alzheimer's disease, and for the past three years this young woman had been her mother's caregiver.

During those years she read all she could about Alzheimer's. One of her takeaways from her research was that there are three fields of endeavor that have been shown to be effective in preventing or at least slowing the onset of the disease: Studying mathematics, learning a foreign language, and creating art. She chose photography as the art medium she wanted to explore and signed up for a photo workshop in Death Valley.

During the first couple of days of the workshop, I noticed that she struggled to learn both composition and the technical aspects of photography. I also noticed that she often separated herself from the group. She wanted to create her own images, and she needed time for herself.

During a sunrise shoot at Eureka Dunes, I found an area with an interesting dune formation and nice sand patterns. I brought the woman to that area, gave her a few ideas, and went to help other workshop participants.

Later that day, the young woman thanked me for leading her to that place. She said that for the first twenty minutes she just sat there, looking and thinking. And then she began making photographs. She said it was the most peaceful, relaxing, and healing experience she had had in years.

So photography can help us heal and help us find our individual and creative voice.

LINDA D. MARSHALL

We all come to earth with a gift or superpower. Some claim and work with their special gift early in life, while others discover and develop them later in life.

Andrew Bernstein, senior official photographer for the NBA, said he knew from the age of fourteen that he was going to be a photographer. He pursued that passion and artistic vision for his entire life.

I used to admire those with a gift or talent as if they were someone special, with something unique that few others possessed. However, with time and self-exploration, I've come to realize that we all have a gift, our uniqueness that can be activated and cultivated at any stage of life. Most often, this happens when we're ready to discover and accept it.

This gift wants to express itself, be it the gift of song, photography, listening, orating, being a change agent, etc. The "gift" may not be apparent at first, because it can be as subtle as how we see and interpret the world. Think about the incredible range of accomplished photographers, teachers, writers, artists, poets, and scientists. It's limitless.

Each individual brings his or her slant to a story or idea. Gifts aren't scarce, nor are they rationed. Quite the opposite, there are 7.5 billion people on this earth, and each person brings something unique.

Unlike Andrew Bernstein, most people do not fully identify or realize what their creative gift or superpower might be at fourteen years old. Meditation is a tool that can help someone uncover their unique gift, which is so often their superpower.

This piece is designed to take you on a journey show you how you might explore your superpower if it isn't abundantly clear. I'll share a process that I used, while explaining how mindfulness and meditation can help you find your creative voice or superpower. I'll dive into how I've used meditation to help others reduce stress, find peace, and uncover their creative voice.

Every day, I am amazed at the level of creativity and ideas that people have swirling in their heads. Their dreams range from starting a business, to writing a book, to merging their passion and career, to sharing a creative vision of their photography, videography, music, and everything in between.

Great works of art and inventions typically begin with a thought or idea that is subsequently brought to life. The thought-form or new view sometimes results in a new product, services, songs, books, stories, or works of art. If you believe in an abundant universe, then you can buy into the idea that there's sufficient space for the creation of any new thing.

I recently held a three-month program where the attendee's mission centered on "being the dream" of what they wanted in their lives. The catalyst for the program stemmed from hearing people describes phenomenal interests, desires, and ideas. For many, their ideas follow them around like the thought bubble in cartoons, while others successfully birth their thing. In this program, I wanted to experiment with moving people from thought to creation and action.

I pondered the question: Wouldn't it be amazing if more people experienced life from a place of creation instead of fear, scarcity, or lack? This curiosity prompted me to assemble a group of eight people to experiment with using meditation as a tool for connecting with their creative genius.

Keep in mind, just like the readers of this book, my attendees came from various cultural and socio-economic backgrounds, bringing different life experiences and levels of success. The fundamental question was, would they commit to exploring new tools to find their inner voice?

We started the group with a set of questions that you could easily ask yourself:

+ What is your superpower?
+ Are you willing to suspend self-judgment and fear of judgment from others to put yourself on the line and challenge your beliefs about problem solving?

+ Are you ready to dive into uncharted waters where the endgame is to find yourself and your creative voice?

Introducing the concept of meditation was at the core of the program. I must admit, the word meditation is pervasive in our societal lexicon, but meditation isn't clearly understood. For our purposes, it's a practice where you focus your mind on a particular object, thought, or activity to achieve a mentally clear and emotionally calm state. *Psychology Today* once reported that it's estimated that the brain has an average of 25,000 to 50,000 thoughts a day, and guess what? Most of those thoughts are negative. Most of our thoughts are a replay of the past or anticipation of the future.

How much of your time is spent in the present moment? Play with me if you will. Let's pause for two minutes and do the following:

+ Minimize noise
+ Sit comfortably
+ Set your timer
+ Close your eyes
+ Follow your breath, the inhale and exhale, for two minutes

How was that for you? Were you able to follow the breath? How many random thoughts did your brain generate in just two minutes?

As you can quickly see, the brain is a constant generator of thoughts, some of them quite random.

The mind is the conductor and lookout, working to keep us safe from real or imagined hazards. It does this while regulating the amazing biochemical system of the mind-body connection.

So, we want and need as our foundation a healthy, fully functioning brain. It's a problem when that thought machine goes non-stop, and the internal dialogue negatively impacts your emotional and physical well-being. Ongoing stress plants the seeds of illness and blocks our flow of creative ideas. How does your brain act under pressure?

Under stress, it's hard to think straight and tap into new solutions. We hunker down and tend to repeat old patterns while expecting new outcomes. When relaxed, we behave quite differently. When in the flow, we listen and see more deeply. Meditation is one of the mindfulness techniques that help facilitate the connection to the creative flow.

Mindfulness is the basic human ability to be fully present, aware of where we are and what we're doing, and not overly reactive or overwhelmed by what's going on around us. I've built a Mindfulness Pyramid that consists of the following: sleep, stress management (meditation, exercise, spiritual connection), nutrition, healthy relationships, being in nature, practicing joy, and gratitude. On a positive note, photography taps into many of the pillars of mindfulness.

As one learns to quiet the mind via meditation or other tools that take you out of your busy mind, both your body and mind begin to shift to a place of restful awareness. There is increasing scientific research with MRI scans that show that after an eight-week course of mindfulness practice, the brain's "fight or flight" center, the amygdala, appears to shrink. This primal region of the brain, associated with fear and emotion, is involved in the initiation of the body's response to stress. The more you meditate, the more you enlarge the brain's control centers that improve creativity, emotional balance, and executive functioning.

> *"Silence is the great teacher, and to learn its lessons, you must pay attention to it. There is no substitute for the creative inspiration, knowledge, and stability that comes from knowing how to contact your core of inner silence."*
> —DEEPAK CHOPRA

A mindful existence with meditation helps you slow down the thoughts and ultimately see that you are not your thoughts. This thought machine is so connected to our physical bodies that our bodies can't discern whether the stressors are real or just in our minds. Hence, over time there can be health consequences when this overactive mind triggers chemicals and neurons that were designed to help us when faced with real and immediate danger.

Meditation has the benefit of calming the brain through the activation of the prefrontal cortex, which influences creativity, executive functioning, and emotional balance. The net result is that a regular meditation practice calms the body and allows us to relax into the magical space of "just being." Got it?

Now back to my small group experiment, in which only one person had a meditation practice. The group found that meditation, when practiced regularly, helped them tap into moments of silence. Some used their breath, music, a mantra, or guided imagery to travel to their place of stillness. In that space, they realized they were not bound by constraints, ego, or fear. They began to see the world more expansively.

The Ph.D. candidate started to shift her approach to her thesis while a few of the entrepreneurs and creatives saw unique angles to their initial ideas. The group members whose concerns were linked to job and life changes envisioned new approaches for work and life. They tapped into a field of information that they couldn't previously access while being so focused on their problems. We then revisited the superpower they claimed on the first day of class and married that to the new vision of their life, and sparks of new possibilities were ignited.

I was amazed at how the group quickly saw themselves as creative geniuses abounding with ideas for both themselves and the group. My novice meditators joked, "This stuff works." Each determined and continues to acknowledge that the quality of their thinking and mental framework is better when they meditate.

So often we try to solve our problems or expand creative vision from the place of the mind. That approach can offer some movement, as we try to "think it through. "I marvel at how my group, myself, and others find their most significant breakthrough comes inside the meditative space between their thoughts. Tapping into inspiration, innovation, and new ways of seeing the world results in manifesting what once were seemingly impossible dreams.

Here's a real example of how the stillness or space appears every day. Imagine the drummer playing his drum. If they hit the drum without interruption, we would consider it noise. The power of drumming is that there is space in between the beats. How that space is manipulated, elongated, or used can stir the souls of man. Space creates music, or, as a world-renowned cellist, Yo-Yo Ma says, "The music is in between the notes."

As we reflect on photography, space also plays an important role. When our friend Rick Sammon teaches about composition, he speaks to how the photographer's use of space and filling or not filling the frame can dramatically alter the look, feel, and impact of an image.

Similarly, as the space in between your thoughts expands, you connect to the silence of your creative center. Here you get to know your superpower and your creative voice. Your uniqueness allows you to contribute in previously unimagined ways. Meditation can guide you to inspiration, creativity, and a sense of peace that unveils your creative potential, voice, and gift.

You may have another activity that takes you to that space of silence. What transports you to the place where you lose track of space and time? Where is your flow point, the place where the ideas and creativity flow? Is it mowing the lawn, creating a picture, playing the guitar, running, walking, dancing, sitting on the ocean's edge, or communing with nature? Do you leave your flow point with greater calm, reflection, and an expanded worldview? If you have that thing, then I encourage you to practice it more frequently.

Through the ages, the great teachers, religions, and philosophers reference prayer, contemplation, and meditation as practices for silencing the mind. Their lives were far different than ours today, but they knew the value of managing the gray matter or the thoughts in our heads. Connect with the place where you no longer control but allow life to unfold. Where is that place for you?

Remember that we all came with a gift. The way that we've been acculturated, trained, and developed in modern society is so related to job and income. Little is focused on what your gift is and how you use that for your livelihood. Or how you bring your gift to your career, so that the organization leverages your unique gift.

I have often wondered if given the choice of picking a superpower from the superpower supermarket, what would I choose? I really can't answer that because every gift has specialness to it.

However, I now appreciate my superpower is that of a healing communicator, which includes deep listening and speaking. Being present and deep listening influenced my ability to lead while in corporate America and is proving indispensable as I teach and coach.

Meditating has stilled my mind so that I can be present with others. Being present and listening also plays a role when I look at my favorite photographs. Most were formed as I listened with eyes and ears and connected to the subject, which could be a person, mountain, or landscape. It just flows more easily when I connect to the subject at the deepest level.

Many people live in deep-seated frustration because they feel stuck, in a rut, are unfulfilled, and can't figure it out. Some wonder, "Is this all there is to life?" I say, "No." Life is a precious gift, and we were all planted with a seed of power and creative genius designed to make this world a better place. Do you make it better through song, photography, videography, or how you combine it all for storytelling or capturing moments that only happen once?

Many of the readers may be artists who often see the world differently and curate special moments from the timeline of life. Your gift will help us remember places, moments, cultures, and experiences that will evaporate with time. What an awesome responsibility and gift. How might this inspire you to use your camera, lens, and vision to capture a moment that is memorialized forever? How does your superpower influence your work?

I hope I have opened up a few new paths for you to identify and explore your superpower. The world needs your genius, so suit up and share your superpower with the world. And if I can be of assistance, come join me at lindamarshall.org, where we can reawaken the superpower within you.

YOUR MISSION

Don't be shy about reaching out to your friends for help, especially when you are feeling down.

17.

CHANGING LANES

*Just before the caterpillar thought it was going to die, it
became a butterfly.*
— ZEN PROVERB

C hanging lanes, in the context of this book, is about changing
careers.

Before we talk about that, it's important to know that there
is a big difference between a job and a career. We go to a job. We live
a career.

In this chapter, some of my full-time professional photographer
friends will share their stories about how they changed lanes, which I
think will be inspiring to those readers who want to make a career change
in their lives. After they chime in, I'll share my changing lanes story.

But first, keep in mind that many internationally and historically famous
people have changed lanes throughout their lives, starting with changing
majors in college, as I am sure many readers of this book have done.

These lane changers include Charles Darwin, author of *On the Origin
of Species by Means of Natural Selection*, which was published in 1859.

Darwin started out studying medicine at the University of Edin-
burgh. He then switched to Cambridge University to get a Bachelor of
Arts degree, which was needed to become an Anglican parson. After
that, he changed lanes to study mathematics.

Eventually, he found his way on to the *Beagle* and traveled to the Galapagos Islands to collect specimens from which he would eventually develop his theory of evolution by natural selection.

Darwin's superpower (see **Chapter 3: Finding Your Superpower and Inner Voice**) *perhaps* was being extremely well organized, disciplined, and dedicated. All his note-taking and research was key to developing his theory of evolution.

Okay, let's see how some of my friends changed lanes.

Ian Plant

Before I became a full-time photographer, I was a lawyer.

I changed lanes because I love photography and I didn't love being a lawyer. For me, it was as easy as that!

Here's what gave me the courage to make the move: I could imagine my life not being a lawyer, but I couldn't imagine my life not being a photographer.

So, I decided to follow my dream without any fear whatsoever. It is said that there is a fine line between courage and stupidity, and I'm not sure which category I fall into, but in any event, I made the switch fifteen years ago and haven't regretted it even once!

Trey Ratcliff

I was a thirty-five-year-old tech guy when I picked up a camera and immediately became obsessed.

I did not mean to change lanes. I just had never discovered something I was so passionate about. I felt like a little kid.

I had no fear. If you think about the worst thing that can happen, and if you're okay with that, then there is no reason to have fear.

JEFF CABLE

Before I became a full-time photographer, I was a director of marketing in the tech industry.

I changed lanes because I wanted to run my own business/photography is way more fun/I could be more creative/I could travel the world/I could make more money.

Here's what gave me the courage to make the move: I had built a solid business on the side so that the jump was easier. I had more than forty events booked when I leaped.

The only thing I miss is the corporate health insurance. :)

SUSAN DIMOCK

Before I became a full-time photographer, I was a Licensed Clinical Social Worker/psychotherapist in private practice.

I changed lanes because it was high-stress work for me, and I burned out. I needed to focus on the positive and the beauty in the world for a while. My photography was a way for me to do so.

Here's what gave me the courage to make the move: The year before my retirement four people in my life, all my age or younger, died of cancer. I felt a wake-up call deep in my bones. It was time to allow myself to switch gears and move into the creative realm that I craved, even though we would take a big financial hit.

My husband supported the move. It was a leap of faith that things would work out financially and they have. I was learning to make decisions based on joy rather than fear.

RANDY HANNA

Can you recall the day you had to make a critical decision? I certainly remember two very specific days in my life when it comes to photography.

I have always been keenly interested in photography, going back as far as junior high school. I credit my Dad for spiking my interest early on and encouraging me to keep with it, still to this day.

When I arrived in the Seattle area, I fell in love with the underwater world and found myself getting deeply involved with underwater photography. Fast forward a few years and I was teaching underwater photography for a local dive shop. I soon started leading underwater photography tours once or maybe twice a year to the South Pacific for the dive shop. I continued leading these trips as long as I could but upward promotions with the Department of Army meant less and less of my time belonged to me. So, although I always had a camera in my hand, the seriousness of my photography took second fiddle to my work.

Fast forward again to a point in my life that I recall very clearly, still to this day. The day was 25 November 2004, Baghdad, and I was in Iraq. It had been a particularly LOUD day, lasting into the night (no further explanation needed). I recall writing a note to myself that I thought I was ready for a change. I left the note open-ended for that evening, sort of a tease. The next day I added to my note, stating that I wanted to go on a photography safari to celebrate my successful deployment.

It took nearly two years, but in 2006 I was on my first photo safari to Tanzania. It was during this trip—a day on the rim of Ngorongoro Crater—that I realized I could really do this: be a professional photographer. I have always been a leader, coach, and mentor. I knew I could take complex issues and distill them into understandable and actionable words. Why not apply all of this to something I loved and something I knew I would be good at? The following year, I was leading my first photo safari into Tanzania. From there it was off to the races, albeit not without a few setbacks along the way. I kept at it and soon my photography transitioned into a full-time career. Little did I know that the competition would be so intense and the field of experts so vast! Yet, I also discovered the camaraderie among those photographers who believed in the theory of abundance, in the joy of sharing tips, stories, and wisdom.

Today, I get up excited about going to work as never before. Not many people can say they are excited about going to work day after day. Leading photography workshops around the world, talking to other photographers, processing and printing photos—it's all exciting to me still to this day and I hope it never fades.

What does it take to change lanes other than the self-evident courage that everyone talks about? First, take charge of your life. Develop a set of goals and objectives. Make them definable and measurable, otherwise it's just talk. Find a mentor. Continuously solicit feedback on your images. Try to learn something new every day and never stop on your quest to practice what you have learned. Surround yourself with others of like passion. Shoot, shoot, shoot. Nobody has become a well-known and successful photographer by taking just one image. Frequently review your goals and objectives and adjust as needed.

What do I do when I feel like a need an extra push? I take on a special project from time to time, one that I can really sink my teeth into. I approach the project with broadly defined goals and objectives and let them morph as I go along. Above all, I won't give up until the project is finished. One critical component of this special project is reaching out to your mentors or photography coaches for advice. Remember, these photographers have all been there before, so heed their wise counsel.

I recall a famous quote that is often attributed to Ansel Adams: "Snapshots are taken, photographs are created." With no formal training or education in photography, I had to learn what it was to create an image.

Now, go learn, photograph, and create. Others have done it, and you can, too!

DON KOMARECHKA

Before I became a full-time photographer, I was an advertising agency jack-of-all-trades.

I changed lanes because the work was soul crushing, and any creative idea I came up with was changed through so many levels of compliance and bureaucracy that it wasn't even my work in the end.

Here's what gave me the courage to make the move: I had one year left before my wife (then fiancé) graduated from university and we would move in together. In this one year, I had a chance to work my ass off and build a business around my passion while having no bills to pay. This was the only time in my life I saw this happening, and I needed to escape the stress and depression of my "day job."

With the support of family and friends (this support was incredibly important), I took the plunge.

MARTIN BAILEY
Before I became a full-time photographer, I was a senior manager at an IT company.

I changed lanes because I knew that if I didn't make the change when I did, I would regret not doing it for the rest of my life.

Here's what gave me the courage to make the move: I had built an audience and had started to sell out tours and workshops while still in my old job. The model was in place, I just needed to free up more time to put everything I had into my business and make it a success.

PATRICIA DAVIDSON
Before I became a full-time photographer, I was a web administrator at a community college. I did the programming and web design for all the college's websites and social media accounts. I also trained college staff to update their pages.

I changed lanes because I found myself thinking about photography and getting outdoors more and more. I was tired of sitting in front of a computer for so many hours.

Here's what gave me the courage to make the move: I quit my job to travel in an RV full-time in 2015. I figured it was a good way to jump-start being a full-time photographer at that point, because I had already a good income from my photography business that I did part-time on the side.

FRANK DOORHOF

Before I became a full-time photographer, my wife Annewiek and I ran a PC and home theater company. We did that for more than twenty years, until we sold the company in 2013 to focus more on photography.

I changed lanes because I felt I couldn't grow creatively; sales were not for me. I love to create and share information, and I found both in photography

I kept postponing what Rick calls "changing lanes," but my wife and I had to know—for sure—that we could keep our family fed and maintain our lifestyle.

Even after we realized that our dream was possible, we still waited another year or so until we knew it was finally time to follow our hearts.

In all honesty, we should have done it much sooner. But I'm a very careful type of person. If you are thinking about changing lanes, look in all directions, check your "rearview mirror," and make the move carefully.

ED COOLEY

Before I became a full-time photographer, I was a software engineer.

I changed lanes because I had spent enough time in an office.

I dared to make the switch because I had an alternate income source that helped with the transition.

SERGE RAMELLI

Before I became a full-time photographer, I was a salesman selling web solutions to hotels in Paris, France. I changed lanes because I always wanted to do something artistic with my life, and although I was making good money, I was thirty-five years old and I felt that I would arrive at sixty without giving the artist's life a shot. You see, my definition of happiness is creating and following a dream or an ambition.

Here's what gave me the courage to change lanes: I had been waiting for years for some big income "win" to come along so I could make the move. One day I realized that the "win" would probably never happen, so I made the leap of faith.

I'll be honest with you. It was rough for the first two years because I had four children that I had to raise.

As it turned out, through hard work and by believing in myself, the move paid off in so many ways, and in more ways than I ever could have expected. I have no regrets and there is no turning back.

If you have a dream, don't wait—give the artist's life a shot.

DARRELL GULIN

Before I became a full-time photographer, I was an executive vice president for a beverage wholesaler of wine, beer, and alcohol.

Picking up a camera after seeing the wonderful work of my purchasing agent, I was being published in national magazines. After marketing my work on a part-time basis for seven plus years, I left that six-figure-income job and started working full-time as a nature and wildlife photographer.

Convincing my wife was the key, so I did a one-year and a five-year business plan, and we agreed that if I made those goals, I could keep going as a full-time photographer. That now has been almost thirty years ago, and I am still going strong with a passion for creating imagery.

MY TURN

I changed lanes in 1990, after working in a Madison Avenue advertising agency for ten years, during which I suffered from crippling back pain due to my repressed anger at myself for working at a job I did not like. I felt I was not myself: three-piece suit, shined shoes, staff meetings, meeting reports, and lots of BS. I talk about all that pain and how I was cured by Dr. John E. Sarno in my *Photo Therapy* book.

Like my friend Ed Cooley, I had spent enough time at a desk. Five years into the job, I started to make an escape plan, with one goal being having what my accountant calls a *cush*—a cushion in the bank to keep me afloat for three years in case things did not work out.

I also wrote books and articles under different names (Richard Michaels and Richard Trout) because if I had used my real name, I would have been fired, and I was not financially ready for that.

And like Frank and Susan Dimock, I had support from my best friend in life, Susan Sammon.

I have changed lanes a few times and have had a few detours in my life. I started as a musician, attending Berklee College of Music in Boston. Then I changed lanes to be the editor of *Studio Photography* and *Photo Processing* magazines. Then came the detour of the ad agency. And today I am weaving in and out of the photography and music lanes, playing music every day.

So, my message to you is this: it's okay to look for signposts up ahead, and to find the best lane for you.

Some photographers I know feel as though they were born to be photographers. I'm not one of them, by the way. But the concept of being born for a certain career is, for sure, something to consider. It's the concept that author Chris Guillebeau explores in his best-selling book *Born for This*, which I highly recommend.

The book has several quotes from people who Chris talked to about their careers. Here's one of my favorites, which I think will help you if and when you consider changing lanes.

"For a long time I thought I should find some passion. Now I realize that passion is not uncovered, it is created. But most people never put in the effort required to get good at something to the point where you grow to love it. I think the passion myth is the number one reason why my friends are miserable at their jobs." —Melodie, age twenty-five, systems and processes architect.

I'd like to leave you with one more lane-changer story. Several years ago a young, part-time photographer, Chris Smith, came to me for an online "tough love" portfolio review session. His full-time job was high school physics teacher. When I saw his website, I said: "Chris, you are a wonderful photographer. You do not need my photo advice. I will, however, give you some career advice. You should be a professional photographer and run photo workshops as I do."

Chris took my advice. He quit his job and started running workshops in Chicago. That turned into Out of Chicago, a major photo event. Since then, Chris has expanded with Out of Oregon, Out of Yosemite, Out of Moab, Out of Costa Rica, Out of Acadia, and is planning for more "Out of" events.

Chris does not take as many photographs as he used to, but he loves running the events.

The message here is that even if you don't change lanes to become a full-time professional photographer, there are other photo lanes into which you can move that can be very fulfilling.

YOUR MISSION
Change lanes carefully. Look in all directions for openings and obstacles.

18.

THE BUSINESS OF
BEING CREATIVE

Dad, I think you're actually an entrepreneur
who happens to be a photographer.
— MARCO SAMMON

We touched briefly on the business side of photography and of being an artist in **Chapter 2: What's Needed on the Photo Artist's Palette?** Let's dive a bit more into that all-important topic.

But first, the opening quote for this chapter is an excerpt from a conservation I had at a local party.

My neighbor: "Rick, what do you do?"

Me: "I'm a photographer."

My son Marco: "Dad, I think you're actually an entrepreneur who happens to be a photographer."

My son made this analysis because he saw how much time I spent on the business side of my photography.

Back in my scuba diving days, there were people we called "dolphin huggers." These individuals loved dolphins. They wanted to protect the dolphins' environment and were out to save the marine world...without having a solid plan or strategy to make that happen. They published pretty pictures of pretty dolphins in pretty environments with the hope that action would be taken to protect these wonderful sea creatures.

For sure, their pictures created a greater awareness of the beauty, and in some cases intelligence, of dolphins. But lacking a business, management, and enforcement plan—such as those enacted by groups like Greenpeace, Ocean Conservancy, the Nature Conservancy, Coral Reef Alliance, and the Sea Shepherd Conservation Society, to name a few—the "dolphin huggers" efforts were not as effective as the efforts of business-minded groups.

Also, back in the scuba diving days, we had a saying: Plan your dive and dive your plan. The idea is that one must make a plan for where and how long to dive, and then follow that dive pattern.

Let's see how this relates to you and your photography. If you are a painter or musician, you will see how these concepts apply to you.

First, you need a business, management, and enforcement plan. All the successful photographers I know have these plans. Likewise, I know some super-talented photographers who, like the "dolphin huggers," want to save the world with their photography, but because they are not good business people, they either can't keep up with their photography and/or can't reach a wide audience.

There are countless books, classroom sessions, and online classes on becoming a good businessperson. I'd suggest making it a top priority to learn the business side of your hobby or craft.

One book I'd recommend to you is *Free: The Future of a Radical Price*, by Chris Anderson. Like it or not, part of being a good businessperson, especially a photography businessperson, is to give stuff away for free—which is discussed in-depth in the book.

When he was alive, my dad asked me one day, after seeing my free videos on YouTube, "Why do you give away so much stuff for free?" I responded, "The more I give away, the more my audience grows, which translates to book and online class sales, as well as workshop and seminar sign-ups."

Unmesh Dinda is a wonderful example of someone who gives a lot of stuff away online for free, which translates to the Photoshop artist being in top demand at Photoshop events. At last count, his YouTube channel, PiXimperfect, has more than 1.85 million viewers, all of whom get to learn for free.

Second, plan your dive (your dive into the business side of your photography) and dive (work hard) into your plan.

All my successful photographer friends and I have something in common when it comes to our business: we spend way more time on the business side of photography than we do on photography. That business time includes, but is not limited to: marketing our work, posting on social media, reading contracts, working to get and keep sponsors, invoicing, networking, and setting and changing business goals. Looking at the business side of other photographers also plays into the plan.

As with our photography, the business side of photography can be very frustrating. However, if we accept the fact that it's part of our photo life and photo quest, when things don't go exactly as planned, we can forge forward, knowing that without a plan, we might be like a "pixel hugger."

In my *Photo Therapy* book, I used a quote by Ernest Hemmingway: "Never confuse movement with action" Basically, Hemmingway is suggesting that there is a difference between making progress and spinning your wheels.

Here I'd like to talk about a somewhat related concept: the Pareto Principle. The Pareto Principle is named after Italian economist Vilfredo Pareto, who in 1906 noticed that 80 percent of the land in Italy was owned by 20 percent of the population. In other words, it's the 80/20 effect: 80 percent of the results come from 20 percent of the causes.

When thinking about the time you spend on different aspects of your business, keep the Pareto Principle in mind, as well as Hemmingway's suggestion. Focus on what is producing the best results for you, and from whom.

Having a trusted business partner is an invaluable asset. I have Susan Sammon, Scott Kelby has Kalebra Kelby, and Harry Benson—known for his Beatles and celebrity photographs—has Gigi Benson.

I worked with Harry and Gigi from 1980 to 1990, when I headed up the Minolta PR account. Harry was a Minolta camera shooter at the time, and we promoted him and his work. I am still friends with them today.

Harry and Gigi are a wonderful example of the value of a trusted business partner. If you have not seen it, look up the 2016 Harry Benson movie, *Harry Benson: Shoot First*. Gigi is in the movie, and you'll see why she is a tremendous asset to Harry.

By the way, although Gigi manages their business, Harry knows the difficulty of the business side. When he's asked at events for his advice for beginning photographers, he says, tongue in cheek, "Buy a guitar." He goes on to say that if a young person wants fame by becoming a photographer, it's easier to be a musician.

YOUR MISSION
Plan your dive into your business and dive into your business plan with passion.

19.

LESSONS LEARNED
IN THE RAIN FOREST

*Anyone who stops learning is old, whether at twenty or
eighty. Anyone who keeps learning stays young.*
— HENRY FORD

I am writing the final text for this book shortly after returning from
spending a week in the rain forest on the Osa Peninsula in Costa
Rica, which National Geographic calls "the most biologically intense place on earth."

Photographing the wildlife (most often far away, backlit, and sur-
rounded by leaves and branches) was an amazing, and for sure challenging, experience.

For me, the most important part of the experience was realizing how
animal behavior and the environment could be related to our lives and
our creative photo quest.

Before I go on, I need to give my friend Ron Clifford credit for this
"relating nature to humans and our photography" concept. You see, in
my *Photo Therapy* book, Ron writes about lessons he learned in Antarctica that apply to one's photography—and life. Ron talks about the pen-
guins (they strive together in harsh conditions), icebergs (they can glow
from within and have a tipping point), and storms (tough times make

us tougher). So, thank you Ron for the inspiration.

Take a look at the lessons I learned in the rain forest and see what they teach us.

LESSONS LEARNED FROM THE LEAFCUTTER ANTS

Leafcutter ants lead a fascinating life. Each day, countless numbers of these "farmer ants" leave their underground nest, march off in clearly defined lines to a nearby plant, chew off a part of a leaf (which can be ten times their body weight), and carry it back to the nest. Once back home, the ants chew the leaves into a pulp that is used to cultivate tufts of nutritious fungus, their food source.

One lesson: the ants work as a team for the common goal of the colony.

The lesson we could learn from the ants: we are all in this together; we need to share and share alike. The successful photographers I know share their contacts and secrets with their fellow photographers, realizing that (to use an old expression) "you meet the same people on the way up as you do on the way down."

These photographers also help each other promote each other's projects on social media. Here, too, what goes around comes around. Plus, it's good karma to share.

Another lesson: the ants don't "think" about the seemingly impossible task of carrying something so heavy that for me, at a weight of two hundred pounds, would be like carrying a two thousand-pound tripod in my teeth. The ants just do it.

This is a good lesson for us. In challenging situations, we often need to "just do it." One technique for accomplishing this goal is to think of a potential problem as a challenge rather than a problem, or to look at the glass as half full rather than half empty.

Also keep this quote in mind: "Aerodynamically, the bumble bee shouldn't be able to fly, but the bumble bee doesn't know it so it goes on flying anyway." —Mary Kay Ash

LESSONS LEARNED FROM THE SLOTHS

Sloths, which spend most of their lives hanging upside down in trees, are the slowest moving mammal on the planet. They take it slow, among other reasons, to conserve energy.

Remember the opening line in the **About This Book** section? It is: "Slow down."

One lesson we can learn from the sloth: slowing down can be a good thing. If we slow down, we can have more energy to be creative and may make fewer mistakes when we are photographing.

Another lesson: hang in there when the going gets tough. I know as well as anyone about the rollercoaster ride of being a photographer— the highs are high and the lows are low. We just need to hang in there until *we* make a change, or as Zig Zigler says, "You don't drown by falling in water; you only drown if you stay there."

LESSONS LEARNED FROM THE WHITE-FACED CAPUCHIN MONKEYS

White-faced capuchin monkeys scurry around the treetops looking for food. If they can't walk or swing to a branch, they take a giant leap— seeming to fly through the air with the greatest of ease—to their target branch. I have seen this dozens of times and the monkeys never miss their mark.

The lesson we can learn here has been attributed to Margaret Shepherd: "Sometimes your only available transportation is a leap of faith."

We need to have faith in ourselves, to believe in ourselves. Sure, making a leap (perhaps changing lanes as I talked about earlier in this book) can be scary. It's like standing at the end of a high diving board at a swimming pool. The longer you stand there and look down, the scarier it gets. But once you make the leap, all your fears are gone. Sure, you might make a belly flop, but if you do, you know what you did wrong and will not make the same mistake again.

We need to take chances and risks in life, and in our photography, to get ahead.

Another lesson: white-faced capuchin monkeys have what's called, "situational awareness." That is, they are keenly aware of everything that is going on around them, including the sounds of other monkey and birds that could warn of predators.

As photographers, we need to have situational awareness so we can be ready to take a picture at a moment's notice if the light and scene changes.

As individuals, we must have situational awareness so we can be prepared for the unexpected, and to be prepared for opportunities that present themselves to us.

Lesson Learned From the Butterflies

Butterflies go through an amazing metamorphosis, starting out as a crawling sack of goo and then transforming into what some call a "flying flower."

The lesson: we can change, or as Dr. Wayne Dyer said in his book, *Real Magic: Creating Miracles in Everyday Life*, we can create our own reality.

The key is to be aware of our actions and how they affect us as well as others—not only now, but in the future. So, trying to see into the future (the ability to anticipate the outcome of one's actions) could be a very useful inner superpower.

You'll find much more about superpowers in **Chapter 3: Finding Your Superpower and Inner Voice**. Don't miss that chapter, because I know you have a superpower, and it's important to discover it.

Lessons Learned From Hummingbirds

Hummingbirds are the only birds that can fly like a helicopter: they can move up, down, sideways, forward, and backward. Upon arriving at a flower, they take a quick sip of nectar, back off, sometimes they return to the same flower after a while, or they are gone in a flash.

One lesson: as photographers, when we see a unique scene or when the light unexpectedly changes, we need to be able to move quickly and easily, with all our gear, into position to get a shot, even when using a tripod and other accessories.

Once in position, we need to be able to make camera adjustments effortlessly, without having to fumble with buttons and dials. Yes, it's good to slow down so you don't make a mistake, but not to the point where you are a sloth to the photographers with whom you are photographing.

More importantly, when you are photographing a person, especially a stranger in a strange land, you never want to overstay your welcome. Like a hummingbird, you want to work fast: get your shot, show the subject your photograph, say thank you, and move on.

Another lesson: a hummingbird often goes back to the same flower again and again to get the most nectar out. As a photographer, if we go back to the same location again and again to get the shot—a different and more creative shot—we can grow photographically.

I follow this practice by going back again and again to the New Croton Dam (five minutes from my home) in Croton on Hudson, New York. I tell myself, "I'm not leaving here without a different image." That image can be created by using a different lens, choosing a different camera angle, using different camera settings, experimenting with a different neutral density filter, photographing at a different time of day or night, or by photographing in different weather conditions.

By now you know I like quotes. Here are a few more that I put into the category of Life Lessons We Can Learn from Mother Nature. Most also relate to our personal photo quest.

There are many quotes here. Maybe you want to come back to this chapter from time to time (like a hummingbird) to read—and to digest—just a few at a time.

No flower blooms for a thousand days.
— CHINESE PROVERB

God is really only another artist. He invented the giraffe, the elephant, and the cat. He has no real style. He just keeps on trying other things.
— PABLO PICASSO

The only Zen you find on the tops of mountains is the Zen you bring up there.
— ROBERT PIRSIG

Between our birth and death we may touch understanding, as a moth brushes a window with its wing.
— CHRISTOPHER FRY

Don't cry when the sun is gone, because the tears won't let you see the stars.
— VIOLETA PARRA

When I judge art, I take my painting and put it next to a God-made object like a tree or flower. If it clashes, it is not art.
— PAUL CÉZANNE

"We think too small, like the frog at the bottom of the well. He thinks the sky is only as big as the top of the well. If he surfaced, he would have an entirely different view."
— MAO ZEDONG

Constant dripping hollows out the stone.
— LUCRETIUS

*There are many paths to the top of the mountain, but the
view is always the same.*
— CHINESE PROVERB

*What is man without the beasts? If all the beasts were gone,
man would die from a great loneliness of the spirit. For
whatever happens to the beasts, soon happens to man.*
— CHIEF SEATTLE

It is not only fine feathers that make fine birds.
— AESOP

Every animal knows more than you do.
— NEZ PERCE PROVERB

Fear an ignorant man more than a lion.
— TURKISH PROVERB

Smooth seas do not make skillful sailors.
— AFRICAN PROVERB

*There is nothing in a caterpillar that tells you
it's going to be a butterfly.*
— RICHARD BUCKMINSTER FULLER

A turtle travels only when it sticks out its neck.
— ANONYMOUS

We can only appreciate the miracle of a sunrise if we have
waited in the darkness.
— ANONYMOUS

YOUR MISSION
Keep the following quote by Zig Ziglar in mind: "You don't have to be great to start, but you have to start to be great."

20.
ALL TOGETHER NOW

Success is the sum of details.
— HARVEY S. FIRESTONE

I could have named this chapter, "Lessons I Learned by Playing Bass Guitar that Apply to Your Photography," but I realize that not many readers play bass guitar, so some of you may have skipped over the chapter.

These lessons are important, and I'll get to them in a moment. For now, however, I'd like to share a poem by Fernando Pessoa that relates to my thinking about putting it all together— by which I mean, applying all the lessons in this book on your personal photo quest.

To be great, be whole.
Exclude nothing.
Exaggerate nothing that is not you.
Be whole in everything.
Put all you are into the smallest thing you do.
So, in each lake, the moon shines with splendor because it
blooms up above.

Being whole, putting it all together, is what makes one a good photographer, bass player, artist, and so on.

Let's take a look at what a bass player needs to put together to be whole, and then let's take a look at what a photographer needs to be whole. You'll see that learning both "instruments" have "need to know" elements. (Hey, maybe this chapter will also inspire you to take up the bass or another musical instrument!)

A Good/Whole Bass Player Needs To:

- Tune his or her instrument before playing.
- If you are right-handed, develop calluses (thick pads of skin on the left-hand fingertips) so the notes sound clean.
- If you are right-handed, develop calluses on the thumb, index, and middle fingers on the right hand so plucking the string does not cause blisters.
- Develop muscles and muscle memory to keep on truckin', so to speak.
- Learn the position of the notes on the fret board.
- Be able to play the notes without looking.
- Develop a good hand position (which is different when playing rock and jazz).
- Know how to adjust the tone with the knobs on the bass.
- Know how to adjust the tone with the knobs on the amp.
- Be able to memorize songs.
- Be able to visualize how the next note or notes will sound.
- Know some tricks, like playing "ghost" notes and chromatic lead-ins to notes.
- Listen to other bass players to see how they play.

- Take bass lessons, either in person or online.
- Listen to critics and take suggestions.
- Practice. A lot!
- "Never confuse movement with action," as Ernest Hemmingway said. In other words, don't keep playing the same well-learned patterns over and over. Rather, learn new patterns—try something different.
- Think about the difference between hearing and listening. One can hear a song without actually listening to the notes.
- Consider the space between the notes and not just the notes themselves. That space is just as important as the notes.
- Get a good instrument. I first bought a cheap bass guitar; one month later I traded it in for a much better sounding and playing bass.
- Get out there and perform—in person and on social media.

A Good/Whole Photographer Needs to Know the Following:

If you are a painter or musician or sculptor, I am sure you will see how these qualities apply to your craft.

- Calibrate his or her camera (set) the white balance, color mode, etc.) before photographing. Calibrating a computer monitor and printer is also important.
- Learn what all the buttons and dials on a camera do.
- Be able to adjust camera settings without looking, which is useful when photographing in low light and in the dark.
- Know how accessories, such as ND filters and polarizing filters, can enhance a scene.

- Develop a steady hand position when photographing, which helps avoid camera shake.
- Be in good physical shape so you don't get tired when hiking around taking pictures.
- Be able to visualize how changing camera controls affect the photograph.
- Know some tricks in Photoshop and Lightroom that can enhance a picture.
- Follow other photographers to learn from them.
- Think about the difference between looking and seeing. One can look at a scene without actually seeing the light and shadows.
- Consider the space between the subjects in a scene. That space, which we call separation, is just as important as the elements in the scene.
- Take photography lessons, either in person, on a workshop, at a seminar or online.
- Listen to critics and take suggestions.
- Get a good camera. Sure, cameras don't take pictures, people do, but the better the camera's sensor and the sharper the lens, the better the pictures and enlargements.
- Practice. A lot!
- "Never confuse movement with action," as Ernest Hemmingway said. In other words, don't keep photographing the same thing over and over. Rather, experiment with new techniques on new subjects—try something different.
- Get out there—in person, at an art gallery, on social media, and so on—and perform.
- Review everything in **Chapter 2: What's Needed on the Photo Artist's Palette?**

YOUR MISSION

Have some fun and listen to the Beatles song, "All Together Now." (I know this is not that serious of a mission, but hey, you must have fun, too!)

21.

ALL MISSIONS

Here's a list of the Missions (a.k.a. assignments) in this book. Come back here from time to time if you need a creative challenge, or if you just want to have some creative fun.

Think Like a Painter.

Take a straight photograph of an everyday object, perhaps a piece or a bowl of fruit. In the digital darkroom, try adding some enhancements. Even a blurry vignette, which appears to change the depth-of-field, can make an image look more artistic. If you are a painter, try similar techniques.

Work with Passion, Persistence, and Purpose—and stay curious.

Set a goal to make five photographs that have a sense of mystery. Follow the advice of Norman Vincent Peale: *"It's always too early to quit."*

Always keep the "conversation" of your photograph in mind.

Don't be afraid to create your own reality with your photographs.

Discover your superpower and be aware of its power in your photography and in your everyday life.

Carefully consider the pros and cons of specializing and not specializing. Do what works for you by following your heart.

Enjoy the process, and remember to "shake the tree" every once in a while.

Try not to be too hard on yourself.

Plan your dive into your business and dive into your business plan with passion.

Listen to your audience and speak to it with your mission statement.

Change lanes carefully. Look in all directions for openings and obstacles.

Wherever you go, go with all your heart.

Don't be shy about reaching out to your friends for help, especially when you are feeling down.

Keep this quote by Zig Ziglar in mind when you have a new project in mind: "You don't have to be great to start, but you have to start to be great."

Be aware of your secret weapon at all times, especially when speaking in public and when writing on public forums.

Set a goal of making a fine art photograph and a fine art print.

Look into, not at, your art.

Have some fun and listen to The Beatles song, "All Together Now."

22.
ALL CHAPTER-OPENER QUOTES

In this chapter, I have put together all the opening quotes for each chapter in this book. There are many more inspirational and motivational quotes scattered throughout this book, especially in **Chapter 19: Lessons Learned in the Rain Forest**.

At the end of this chapter you'll also find a quote that is not on the previous pages, a quote sent to me by my good friend Alec Arons.

If you are at lows on the creative rollercoaster, read a quote or two for an "artistic pick-me-up."

"An artist cannot fail; it is a success to be one."
— CHARLES COOLEY

"Every child is an artist. The problem is how to remain an artist once he grows up."
— PABLO PICASSO

"I don't care about the audience; I am the audience."
— LORD SNOWDON

*"Confidence isn't thinking you are better than
everyone else, it's realizing that you have no reason to
compare yourself to anyone else."*
— MARYAM HASNAA

*"Ideas alone can be works of art…All ideas need not be made
physical…A work of art may be understood as a conductor
from the artist's mind to the viewer's. But it may never reach
the viewer, or it may never leave the artist's mind."*
— SOL LEWITT

*"I win in every fight; my secret weapons are my
kindness and forgiveness."*
— DEBASISH MRIDAH

*"We all know that art is not truth.
Art is a lie that makes us realize the truth."*
— PABLO PICASSO

*"Art is filling a space in a beautiful way.
That's what art means to me."*
— GEORGIA O'KEEFFE

"Art is a habit-forming drug."
— MARCEL DUCHAMP

*"Passion is one great force that unleashes creativity,
because if you're passionate about something,
then you're more willing to take risks."*
— YO-YO MA

"Never confuse movement with action."
— ERNEST HEMMINGWAY

"Without discipline, there's no life at all."
— KATHERINE HEPBURN

"Art is a revolt, a protest against extinction."
— ANDRÉ MALRAUX

"When you destroy the mystery of the photograph,
you destroy the photograph."
— UNKNOWN

"I don't care if you make a print on a bath mat,
as long as it's a good print."
— EDWARD WESTON

If you can't make a good print, make a big print.
— PHOTO ADAGE

"It's always too early to quit."
— NORMAN VINCENT PEALE

"Life is a conversation. Make it a good one."
— GLENNON DOYLE MELTON

"The adult is the child who survived."
— URSULA LEGUIN

"Imagination is more important than knowledge."
— ALBERT EINSTEIN

"Batman doesn't have any superpowers. He has to use his brain and his courage. That's what always appealed to me."
— PATRICK LEAHY

"You only have your thoughts and dreams ahead of you. You are someone. You mean something."
— BATMAN

"Be faithful to that which exists nowhere but in yourself— and thus make yourself indispensable."
— ANDRÉ GIDE

"I spent most of my life trying to specialize myself. I went to theater school, film school, music school, mime school, art school…Finally, I was able to gather enough knowledge to build the confidence to create my own work, that goes utterly against the sense of specialization."
— NUNO ROQUE

"The range of human knowledge today is so great that we're all specialists and the distance between specializations has become so great that anyone who seeks to wander freely between them almost has to forego closeness with the people around him."
— ROBERT M. PIRSIG

"One science only will one genius fit."
— ALEXANDER POPE

"Each man is capable of doing one thing well. If he attempts several, he will fail to achieve distinction in any."
— PLATO

"Don't be distracted by criticism. Remember—the only taste of success some people have is when they take a bite out of you."
— ZIG ZIGLAR

"A real friend is one who walks in when the rest of the world walks out."
— ANONYMOUS

"To escape criticism: Do nothing, say nothing, be nothing."
— ELBERT HUBBARD

"Dad, I think you're actually an entrepreneur who happens to be a photographer."
— MARCO SAMMON

"Ideas are like rabbits. You get a couple and learn how to handle them, and pretty soon you have a dozen."
— JOHN STEINBECK

"It's easier to criticize somebody else than to see yourself."
— GEORGE HARRISON

"Successful people will always be attacked in some form or another, and usually by those that lacked the courage to reach for their dream or to make a difference in their lives or the lives of others."
— ANONYMOUS

"Men go abroad to wonder at the heights of mountains, at the huge waves of the sea, at the long courses of rivers, at the vast compass of the ocean, at the circular motions of the stars, and they pass by themselves without wondering."
— SAINT AUGUSTINE

"The only Zen you find on the tops of mountains is the Zen you bring up there."
— ROBERT PIRSIG

"Confidence is contagious. So is the lack of confidence."
— VINCE LOMBARDI

"Optimism is the faith that leads to achievement. Nothing can be done without hope and confidence."
— HELEN KELLER.

Learning is health.
— BUDDHIST SAYING

"I would rather die of passion than of boredom."
— VINCENT VAN GOGH

"The camera is an instrument that teaches people how to see without a camera."
—DOROTHEA LANGE

"To consult the rules of composition before making a picture is a little like consulting the law of gravitation before going for a walk."
— EDWARD WESTON

"When you're curious, you find lots of interesting things to do."
— WALT DISNEY

Just before the caterpillar thought it was going to die,
it became a butterfly.
— ZEN PROVERB

"Anyone who stops learning is old, whether at twenty or
eighty. Anyone who keeps learning stays young."
— HENRY FORD

Creativity is allowing yourself to make mistakes. Art is
knowing which ones to keep."
— SCOTT ADAMS

"Even a true artist does not always produce art."
— CARROLL O'CONNOR

"A photograph is usually looked at and seldom looked into."
— ANSEL ADAMS

"Success is the sum of details."
— HARVEY S. FIRESTONE

Hey all, Rick's friend Alec Arons here. Here's a quote by George Harrison that summarizes the essence of my photo quest, and I hope helps you with yours:

"With every mistake we must surely be learning."

Learning is a source of energy. The quest for many photographers is one of growth and development as we shape our artistic voice.

Have fun, of course, but when you miss the shot or make a mistake slow down and learn from it.

MY BIOS

I f you think "Bios" (plural) is a typo, I don't blame you. But here's the thing: we *all* have more than one bio because we all do several things. For example, my dear friend Scott Kelby is a photographer, workshop instructor, Photoshop/Lightroom expert, and talented musician—as well as a wonderful husband, great dad, and good friend to many. He also is the CEO of KelbyOne and the publisher of *Photoshop User* and *Lightroom* magazines.

Before I share my bios, think about yours: your photography bio, your family bio, your superpower bio, your outdoors life bio, and so on. Take a moment and then come back.

See what I mean? You do many things and are good at many things. Now, take a moment to write down your bios, using only one sentence. I guess that they will help you build your confidence, which I talked about earlier in this book. Okay, here are my bios:

+ Proud dad, whose son is getting his Ph.D. in finance (as I write this book in 2020).
+ Happy husband, married to Susan Sammon for 45 years (as of 2020), with whom he has traveled to about 100 countries.
+ Self-taught photographer, who keeps learning every day.
+ Author, who got an F in typing in 9th grade and who has

written 41 books.

- Online trainer, who loves to teach others how to make good photographs in-camera and in Photoshop.
- Musician, who has a few guitars and who plays jazz every day.
- Guitar and piano teacher, who offers free lessons at "Rick's Music Room" on ricksammon.com.
- Gardener, who when he returns from a trip, cuts the lawn even before he backs up his images.
- Called "The Godfather of Photography" (by some) because he has been around a long time, in addition to the fact that he likes to help other photographers.
- Avid walker, who goes on two 45-minute walks each day (up and down the hills of Croton on Hudson, New York) because he has made being healthy one of his top priorities.
- Magician! Getting back to my friend Scott Kelby, when I went to his house one night for a nice Greek dinner, I spent about 20 minutes doing card tricks (the same ones I do around the world for strangers in strange lands) and my favorite coin trick for his daughter. She thought I was a magician.

Again, my friend, think about all *your* bios, and all the things at which you are good!

PLEASE STAY IN TOUCH

I'd love to stay in touch with you, and I hope you can stay in touch with me. It's always fun and satisfying to hear from readers.

For starters, I'd love to know which chapter or chapters were your favorites. I'd also, of course, be interested to hear how this book has motivated you and helped you to find your photographic and creative voice.

MY WEBSITE
www.ricksammon.com

ON FACEBOOK
https://www.facebook.com/RickSammonPhotography

ON MY FACEBOOK PHOTO THERAPY GROUP

ON TWITTER
https://twitter.com/ricksammon

ON INSTAGRAM
https://www.instagram.com/ricksammonphotography/

Hey! If you feel as though you got a lot out of this book and know someone who would like to go on a creative *Photo Quest*, please spread the word. You can also spread the word by posting a review on Amazon.

Finally, a big "Thank You" for spending some time with me. I truly appreciate it!

www.ingramcontent.com/pod-product-compliance
Lightning Source LLC
Chambersburg PA
CBHW021400210526
45463CB00001B/165